MICHIGAN

in quotes

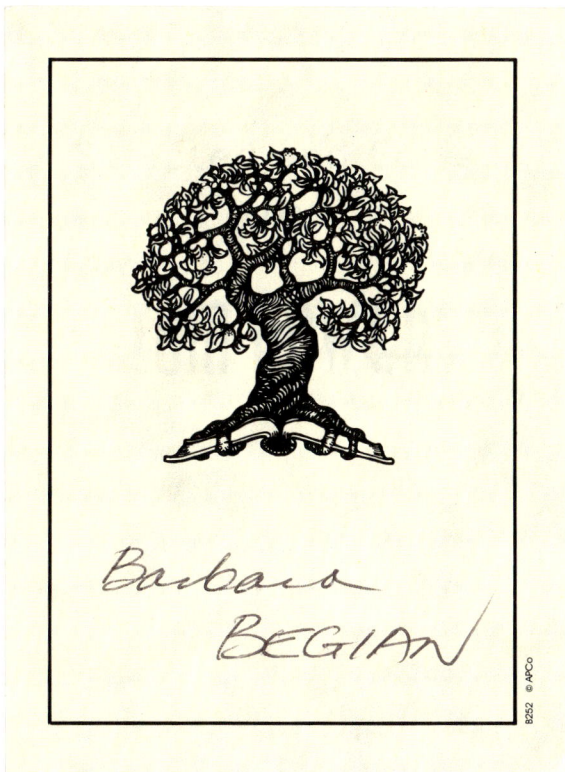

Barbara
BEGIAN

B252 © APCo

Friede Publications

Friede Publications
2339 Venezia Drive
Davison, MI 48423

Printed in the United States of America

First printing, April 1994

ISBN 0-923756-08-6

For
Zachery, Samantha and Bonny.

Your Grandfather looks forward to quoting you ad naseum

Other titles by Tom Powers

Natural Michigan
Michigan State and National Parks: A Complete Guide
More Natural Michigan

Other titles by Friede Publications

Unexplained Michigan Mysteries
Ultimate Michigan Adventures
Michillaneous
Mich-Again's Day
Murder, Michigan
Michillaneous II
Canoeing Michigan Rivers
A Traveler's Guide to 116 Michigan Lighthouses
A Traveler's Guide to 100 Eastern Great Lakes Lighthouses
A Guide to 199 Michigan Waterfalls
Fish Michigan —100 Southern Michigan Lakes
Fish Michigan —100 Northern Lower Michigan Lakes
Fish Michigan —100 Upper Peninsula Lakes

Contents

Author's Note

This book started with a quote that rattled around in the back of my mind for several years. A soldier stationed on Mackinac Island more than a century and a half ago said that the place was so healthy that people had to "leave the island to die."

For a Michigander who fell in love with Mackinac Island when in his teens and whose passion for the place has never waned, the quote not only captured one of the enduring qualities of the enchanted isle but in its own peculiar way helped define Mackinac's essence. Over the years I ran across other equally fascinating quotes about Michigan, but after mentally buffing them like literary Petoskey stones, they slipped from memory.

The thought crossed my mind that it would be fun to collect, compile and share outstanding quotes about Michigan — its cities, natural attractions, fauna and flora, landmarks and the Great Lakes that define our state. I was sure that there were plenty of others who would find as much delight in poignant, trenchant and humorous sayings and observations about Michigan as I did.

The project began as a relaxing diversion but soon grew to obsession. What had been idle pursuit soon consumed nearly every waking moment away from my real job. My schedule was revised to include twice-monthly trips to the state library in Lansing to check out books and pore through reference works. For two years a book or magazine was always in hand, whether I was watching TV, cooking dinner, or lying in bed waiting for sleep to come.

What follows are the best and most memorable excerpts culled from more than 500 sources — novels, journals of early explorers, local histories, nonfiction studies, newspaper articles, travel pieces both past and present, biographies, autobiographies, and even government reports.

The quotes come from the famous — James Fenimore Cooper, Bruce Catton, former Governor Milliken, Henry Schoolcraft, Herman Melville and Mark Twain — as well as the unknown, such as at least one convicted criminal and a nameless miner trying to scratch a living out of the U.P. bedrock. The more than a thousand different views, opinions and images form an intriguing, colorful Michigan mosaic. I hope you find it fun, provocative and endlessly fascinating.

Tom Powers
Flint, Michigan

Architecture

Belle Isle Aquarium

"The building ... is a small marvel. With its arched ceiling of undersea-green tiles, the Belle Isle aquarium has an underwater feel to it. If there's a railroad station in Atlantis it must look something like this."

MARTIN F. KOHN. *Family Fare: A Guide To Fun In And Around Michigan.* 1988

Calumet Opera House

GARY W. BARFKNECHT

"... a veritable gem, admirable in appointments and decorations and worthy of a place on Broadway. ..."

New York theatrical agent E. D. PRICE. 1901

Detroit-Winsdor Tunnel

"The Detroit-Winsdor Funnel."

A common nickname the newly opened tunnel earned in the late 1920s because of the large quantity of whiskey smuggled into Detroit via the tunnel during Prohibition.

Fisher Building

• Designed in 1928 by Detroit architect Albert Kahn, the Fisher Building was the largest commercial structure of its time.

"The treasures of an art museum, the utility of an office building and the majesty of a church combine in Kahn's 'Cathedral to Commerce.' "

ROBERT BRODBECK. *Michigan Living.* February 1986.

"Michigan's largest art work."

DORIS SCHARFENBERG. *Long Blue Edge of Summer.* 1992.

Fox Theater

"Few specimens of architectural splendor, either ancient or modern, surpass the new Fox Theater."

Detroit Free Press. 1928.

"... the greatest and gaudiest of all movie palaces."

ROBERT J. WARSHAM. *Michigan History.* March/April 1980.

Fox Theatre (cont.)

"That it was built for mere movies and not coronations, almost boggles the mind."

RICK SYLVAIN. *Michigan Living*. February 1989.

Grand Hotel
(Mackinac Island)

GARY W. BARFKNECHT

"It's a big white elephant."

Petoskey Independent Democrat. 1893.

"They suggested a bucket be secured, a sterling silver bucket if need be to please my expensive tastes, and that my money be put into it and poured down the sink. This would shorten the ordeal of losing my money and make it much easier."

W. STEWART WOODFILL, telling of the reaction his family had when he announced his purchase of the hotel in 1933.

"It's an aged wooden frame building held together by more coats of paint than one can count."

CHARLES WAGONER, travel editor for the *Detroit Times*. 1950s.

"When you register as a guest you are transported into the Victorian-era as a member of its privileged leisure class. ... There's nothing else like it in the world."

GARY BARFKNECHT. *Ultimate Michigan Adventures.* 1989.

Hudson's

• At 25 stories Hudson's downtown Detroit building was the world's tallest department store until it closed in the early 1980s.

"... fourteen floors of cash registers, every floor the size of a city block."

ELMORE LEONARD. *Swag*. 1976.

"This building was a landmark of Detroit in the same way the Eiffel Tower is of Paris. The news that this institution shall close down is an unbelievable horror."

Architectural planner VICTOR GRUEN. 1980.

Marquette Prison

"Serving time in Marquette Prison, on the shore of the largest freshwater lake in the world, must be like dying on the first day of spring, day after day."

LOREN ESTLEMAN. *Downriver*. 1988.

Northland Shopping Center

• Northland Mall began a retail revolution when it opened in Southfield in 1954 as America's first suburban shopping mall.

"One of the few uniquely American building types, the new trading post in the exurban wilderness. ..."

Architectural critic WOLF VON ECKARDT. 1950s.

Renaissance Center (see p. 4)

Silverdome

"... the monster muffin."

SONNY ELIOT. *Michigan Living*. September 1988.

State Capital Building

STATE CAPITOL TOUR SERVICES

"... a large hand-cut sandstone and granite building topped by a highly visible white dome that points into the downtown Lansing sky like an egg topped by a rocket."

GARY BARFKNECHT. *Ultimate Michigan Adventures*. 1989.

Willow Run Assembly Plant

• The plant was built during World War II to manufacture bombers. The 67-acre main building had a mile-long final assembly line.

"... a sort of Grand Canyon of the mechanized world."

CHARLES LINDBERGH, describing his impression of Willow Run in 1942. *The Wartime Journals of Charles Lindbergh*. 1970.

Renaissance Center

"The brown-and-silver towers of the Renaissance Center rose from the construction surrounding them like feudal ruins. ... Near the site in the year 1701, Cadillac erected a village of stout logs designed to withstand an indian siege, and in 1974 history swung full circle when the city he founded began work on a structure impressive enough to discourage rioters and second-story men. ..."

LOREN ESTLEMAN. *Angel Eyes.* 1981.

"... it's a pretty piece of work and about as necessary as a Tiffany lamp in a home for the blind."

LOREN ESTLEMAN. *Angel Eyes.* 1981.

"The Renaissance Center is akin to the agora of ancient Athens."

Rand McNally. *Guide to Michigan.* 1979.

"... there was the massive dark glass tubes of the Renaissance Center, five towers, the tallest one 700 feet high, standing like a Buck Rogers monument over downtown."

ELMORE LEONARD. *City Primeval: High Noon in Detroit.* 1980.

"Mayor Young's first brainchild and a paean to the parsimony of late-twentieth-century architecture, standing like a display of disposable plastic drinking cups."

LOREN ESTLEMAN. *King of the Corner.* 1992.

"The outside rises like the Emerald City of Oz done up in grey glass, while the interior intriguingly resembles a chain of caverns with sidewalk bazaars in the hollows. ... Getting lost is easier than spending money."

DORIS SCHARFENBERG. *The Long Blue Edge of Summer.* 1992.

Automobiles

"You ask if I have seen any airships yet. I have not, to tell the truth, but there are so many automobiles. They drive with them wherever they go. Soon you can't walk on the roads because of these crazy things."

From a letter written in 1909 by GEORGE ERICKSON of Stambaugh, Michigan, in the Keweenaw Peninsula, to a friend in Sweden.

"The automobile — perhaps more so in Michigan than elsewhere — is regarded as one of the necessaries of life, on par with food, clothing, and shelter."

HARVEY KLEMMER. *National Geographic.* December 1944.

"Detroit did not exactly invent the automobile, but it picked up the thing when it was nothing better than a costly and unreliable toy for the rich and made it a necessity for everybody in America."

BRUCE CATTON. *Holiday Magazine.* August 1957.

"Detroit's not evil, just blind, deaf, and a little stupid. Safe cars are like sensible shoes, harder to sell than the flashy pumps that pinch your toes and ruin your arches."

LOREN ESTLEMAN. *Motown.* 1991. The novel was set in the mid-1960s.

"Invent a simple device like the automobile, to get you from here to there more quickly than you could go without it: before long you are in bondage to it, so that you build your cities and shape your countryside and reorder your entire life in the light of what will be good for the machine instead of what will be good for you.

Detroit has shown us how that works."

BRUCE CATTON. *Waiting for the Morning Train.* 1972.

"The automobile created modern Michigan."

ALAN CLIVE. *State of War: Michigan in World War II.* 1979.

"When the U.S. economy catches a cold, Michigan gets pneumonia."

An old saying from various sources that accurately reflects consumer hesitancy to buy cars during a recession which in turn makes recessions particularly hard felt in Michigan.

"Finding a job in an auto plant today is harder than getting into Harvard."

ZE'EV CHAFETS. *Devils Night and Other True Tales of Detroit.* 1990.

"The Big Three U.S. automakers are now Mattel, Matchbox and Tonka."

JAY LENO. *Detroit Free Press.* March 8, 1992.

"GM Cuts, Michigan Bleeds."

Detroit Free Press. February 25, 1992. The front-page headline reported on GM cuts and plant closings that cost Michigan 9,000 jobs.

"Hell, I didn't go to Japan to help open the rice market. The last time I looked, we don't grow any rice in Detroit."

LEE IACOCCA, president of Chrysler Motors. From a speech to the Economic Club of Detroit calling for continued U.S. pressure to open more trade between Japan and Detroit. January 10, 1992.

Bridges

Ambassador Bridge
....

"... a short ride for a dollar."

WILLIAM SAROYAN. *Short Drive, Sweet Chariot.* 1966.

"Reaching skyward, its magnificent towers give the populace of Detroit and Windsor, as well as traveling newcomers, a sight perhaps as awe inspiring as that witnessed by Father Louis Hennepin, the Jesuit priest, who reported on the remarkable beauty of the natural Detroit River scene more than three hundred years ago."

PHILIP MASON. *Ambassador Bridge.* 1987.

Mackinac Bridge

"In their winter lodges before white men came into the country, the Chippewas told of a great chief who gathered stones on the Lake Huron shore and made a path across the northern narrows. Their legend describes an autumn storm that broke the bridge and carried the stones away — except those that remained as Bois Blanc, Round and Mackinac Islands."

WALTER HAVINGHURST. *Three Flags at the Straits.* 1966.

"What this area needs is a bridge across the Straits."

COMMODORE VANDERBILT, at the dedication of the Grand Hotel on Mackinac Island. 1882.

"You could look out at the empty straits, just five miles wide and hundreds of feet deep, ... and it was inconceivable that they could put a bridge across it."

JIM HARRISON. *Sundog.* 1984. The novel was set during the 1950s.

"I confess that I was awed by my first view of the vast expanse of water to be bridged. One shore was hardly visible from the other. My awe turned into a silent prayer."

DAVID B. STEINMAN, designer of the Mackinac Bridge. 1950.

"You might as well try to build a bridge on the moon. The Straits area is a hundred miles from nowhere. There isn't enough traffic to justify the cost. How do you expect a backwoods bridge to pay for itself."

WILLIAM RATIGAN. *Straits of Mackinac.* 1957. The author was summarizing arguments against building the bridge.

"The bridge we're building should last as long as the pyramids of Egypt lasted ... and then some."

GROVER C. DENNY, the engineer in charge of constructing the bridge's substructure. 1950s.

"... the conquering of the impossible."

WILLIAM RATIGAN. *Straits of Mackinac..* 1957.

"A poem in steel."

DAVID B. STEINMAN. 1950s.

"... at the back of beyond, at the jumping-off place of creation, here, far from major centers of population, to find the world's greatest suspension bridge and longest over-water crossing on the globe, this was a surprise. The Mackinac Bridge jumped out of nowhere and shouted: Boo!"

WILLIAM RATIGAN. *Straits of Mackinac.* 1957.

"Even if I never amount to a dime or do a lick of work again, I can live proud the rest of my days, and brag to my great-grandchildren, about how I had a hand in building the Mackinac Bridge."

An anonymous bridge worker quoted in *Highways Over Broad Waters* by WILLIAM RATIGAN. 1959.

"Mackinac Bridge paved a way into the rambunctious Northwoods, not into a polite little metropolitan park with a bowl of goldfish in the middle."

WILLIAM RATIGAN. *Straits of Mackinac.* 1959.

"It has become a new Northwest Passage."

The Great Lakes: North America's Inland Seas. 1974.

"... a symbol of unity for this most pecu-

liarly shaped state."

NOEL GROVE. *National Geographic.* June 1979.

"Why would anyone build the most spectacular bridge in the world at the top of Michigan instead of at Detroit where everyone could see it?"

From an irate taxpayer's letter to the governor of Michigan. 1980.

"The first time you sail a boat under the bridge crossing the Straits of Mackinac it will be one of your greatest thrills asea, and it is not much less of a thrill in subsequent passages."

JOHN B. TORINUS. *Summer Sail II.* 1985.

"Had the bridge been financed in 1983 it would have required a bond issue of $350,000,000 at an interest rate of 10 percent. ... To pay off this bond issue the bridge fare would have been about $30 per vehicle."

LAWRENCE RUBIN, Executive Secretary of the Mackinac Bridge Authority. 1985. A $96 million bond issue paid for the 1957 construction, and the toll for a car is $1.50.

"... the best thing that could happen to the U.P. would be for somebody to bomb the bridge."

JOHN VOELKER, former Michigan Supreme Court justice and the author of *Anatomy of a Murder.* Voelker was afraid the bridge would destroy his beloved U.P. wilderness. This quote was first voiced during the late 1950s and reported in the April 1990 issue of *Michigan Living.*

"... it's estimated less than 50 percent of state residents have ever seen the bridge. That's like living in Washington D.C., and never visiting the Washington Monument."

BILL SEMION. *Michigan Living..* April 1991.

(Old) Zilwaukee Bridge

• The Zilwaukee Draw Bridge, which carried I-75 over the Saginaw River until 1987, was the only spot along the 1,800-mile-long interstate connecting Tampa Bay, Florida, to Sault Ste. Marie where traffic was regularly stopped. When the bridge was raised on summer weekends to let a ship pass up or down the river, traffic often backed up for 15-20 miles.

"... this bascule span has been a bigger vacation spoiler than ants in your picnic basket, rain at your beach party ... or your car running out of gas and getting two flat tires at the same time."

JERRY CHESKE. *Motor News.* June 1970.

"Cursed at, rammed by two ships, struck by numerous autos, linked to hundreds of injuries and several deaths, the Zilwaukee Bridge has stood as a monument to all that is bad for man and his automobile."

JERRY CHESKE. *Motor News.* June 1970.

FLINT JOURNAL

(New) Zilwaukee Bridge

• During the late 1970s, construction began on a new bridge that was to replace the infamous Zilwaukee Draw Bridge. On August 28, 1982, as a 150-ton section was being added to the world's largest precast concrete segmental bridge, the bridge cracked. The structural failure doubled the initial cost to $117 million and delayed completion of the project for four years.

"It's a name that has become synonymous with bungled projects on a mind boggling scale. It's a suburb that lent its name to a bridge that sends shivers through Michigan Highway officials everywhere. It's Zilwaukee."

Detroit Free Press. January 7, 1987.

"... the new Zilwaukee Bridge, still unfinished after five years, rising like Roman ruins out of the low thumb area. ..."

LOREN ESTLEMAN. *Downriver.* 1988.

FLINT JOURNAL

Cities

Adrian

"... one of the most flourishing villages in Michigan."

Michigan Gazetteer. 1838.

"... in 1874 the settlement of 10,000 supported over fifty saloons and four breweries. No expenditure by the city council for street lights in Adrian was necessary until the twentieth century, since the streets were brightly illuminated all night by bright lights of the saloons."

LARRY ENGELMANN. *Michigan History*. Summer 1977.

Alpena

"A person approaching Alpena from the bay, the first time, will not be much impressed by the scene before him, especially if he is artistically inclined."

WILLIAM BOULTON. *Complete History of Alpena County*. 1876.

"The streets (of Alpena) are paved with sawdust, or pulverized plank as they are jocosely termed. ... The greatest fault that is found with the patent pulverized pavement is its great inclination for visiting — its greatest desire being to get on some other street, and it is nothing uncommon to see half a dozen streets so badly mixed up by the wind, that even the Street Commissioner is unable to tell which is which."

WILLIAM BOULTOUN. *Complete History of Alpena County*. 1876.

"Most tourists would hardly care to linger about Thunder Bay or in the desolation of the region through which recent forest fires have raged."

CLIFTON JOHNSON. *Highways and Byways of the Great Lakes*. 1911.

Ann Arbor

"Our water is the purest limestone, the face of the country moderately uneven, our river the most beautiful I have beheld, and abounding with the most valuable fish, climate is as pleasant as tis possible to be. ..."

JOHN ALLEN, one of the founders of Ann Arbor, indulging in a bit of promotion in 1825, one year after founding the town.

"... the land is laid into to(o) small lots for so inland a place and held at the most extravagant prices. There is some good timbered land in the Neighborhood but this is the poorest part of Michigan I have seen."

From the diary of SALMON KEENEY, a traveler to the Michigan Territory. 1825.

"... Ann Arbor was at the extreme west end of the habitable world, beyond which the sun went down into a boundless, bottomless morass, where the frightful sound of yelling indians, howling wolves, croaking frogs, rattling massaugers, and buzzing mosquitoes added to the awful horror of the dismal place."

HENRY LITTLE, an early pioneer of Kalamazoo County recalling the settling of Michigan in the 1830s. *Michigan Pioneer and Historical Collection.* Vol III, 1881.

"The little town of Ann Arbor looks freshly carved and painted, as if it had stepped out of a Nuremburg toyshop only yesterday."

KARL NEIDHARD, a German visitor to Ann Arbor in 1835.

"... one of the most pleasant and flourishing inland towns in the state."

Michigan Gazetteer. 1838.

"Ann Arbor is a delightful place of about two or three thousand inhabitants and is in every respect a much neater and more thriving place than any of its size in our state. ... I do not wonder that people are made crazy by coming to Michigan if what I see is a specimen of the country."

From the pioneer journal of New Yorker, LANSING B. SWAIN in 1841.

"People are beginning to see that our city is the most desirable place in all the West for residences, as well as business."

Local News and Advertiser editorial. September 1858.

"Every town cannot be a manufacturing place. Our city is a literary city and as such we are proud of it. ..."

Ann Arbor Peninsular Courier. 1870.

"... if it were not for the University, Ann Arbor would be dead."

Ypsilanti Sentinel. 1875.

"In Ann Arbor it is more of a crime to beg than to steal."

Stockbridge Sun. 1880s.

"I have been to all the principal Universities of the United States. At Cambridge where Harvard is situated, there are no saloons allowed, but in Ann Arbor, the places are thick where manhood is drugged and destroyed."

CARRIE NATION. 1899.

"Athens of the West."

KENNETH MILLAR. *The Dark Tunnel.* 1944.

Bad Axe

"... a small city with a strange name."

JAMES RUDIN. *Michigan History.* Summer 1972.

Battle Creek

"Battle Creek citizens (during the 1860s) firmly believed that when General Lewis Cass said, 'If you would seek a pleasant peninsula, look about you' ... that Cass was thinking of the spot where the 'crick' joins the Kalamazoo River, deep in the heart of Battle Creek.

GERALD CARSON. *Michigan History.* September. 1957.

"Cereal Bowl of America."

Michigan Historical Marker. Kellogg, Post and forty other cereal manufacturers put Battle Creek on the map in the early 1900s, and the town became synonymous with breakfast cereal.

"... the best known city of its size in the world."

ROGER L. ROSENTRETER, referring to the early 1900s. *Michigan History.* May/June 1980.

"Named for a ruckus between two Indians and two surveyors, one of the world's most minuscule Indian affrays, in which no wounds worse than a broken head were inflicted. ..."

GERALD CARSON. *Michigan History.* September 1957.

Bay City

"Who would then have thought a city would one day stand where there was but a swamp, with long grass, in which a man could stand and be hid — where there was scarcely an opening in the woods around it, in which the wolves made plenty of howling."

LEON TROMBLE, who in 1831 was the first settler to build a log cabin on the present site of the city. Tromble abandoned it within a year.

"The first pavement in Bay City was made of pine blocks that floated away during high water after a winter of deep snow."

WALTER HAVINGHURST, describing the city in the 1880s. *The Long Ships Passing.* 1943.

"The rapid growth since Civil War times has often brought the remark it is sure to become a second Chicago on the Great Lakes, and ready to claim its space as one of the great cities in our nation."

Cities on the Bay. 1888.

"Here were found every facility for drunkeness, debauchery and gambling, all or singly, associated with deeds of robbery and even murder. Here, in the darkness made visible by the flare and glare of dirty lamps, day and night alike, were found congregated the lowest and most degraded of both sexes. Here, the most horrible obscene orgies were carried on with perfect impunity — for woe to the officer who alone would attempt a 'raid' upon the 'Catacombs,' it was virtually as much as his life was worth."

JOHN FITZMAURICE. *The Shanty Boy or Life on a Lumber Camp.* 1899. The Catacombs was the worst of the many saloons and bordellos that flourished in Bay City during the lumbering era.

"Bay City has become a jewel of restored buildings. ... Driving into ... (it) is like entering a bit of what America used to be."

MEGAN SWOYER. *Michigan Living.* June 1988.

Bay View

"About thirty cottages are now on the ground, some of the them very neat costing anyway from $200 to $600."

SETH REED, Secretary, Bay View Association. 1878.

"Nothing has been neglected to make Bay View fragrant with pleasant and invigorating influences."

Grand Adventure. 1912.

"Michigan's Brigadoon. ... Every summer it rubs its tired turn-of-the-century eyes and opens up the 400 front-porch doors that have not been opened since the previous September."

MILAN STETT. *Motor News.* July 1961.

Bellaire

"All are invited to participate in having a good time (at Bellaire's first Fourth of July Celebration). Competent guides with compasses, axes, and all the necessary appliances for getting through swamps will be furnished free of expense, also an escort armed with shot guns will accompany each party to keep off the musquitoes."

An advertisement in an 1879 issue of the *Traverse Bay Progress*, Elk Rapids. The people of Elk Rapids were obviously upset that the county seat had been moved from their village to the swampy, wooded, uncivilized and "imaginary" town of Bellaire, in the center of Antrim County.

Benton Harbor

"We went over to Uncle Sam Russell's 'Eden,' which has a fine map of land laid out into cities and is called North St. Joseph. Nothing could induce me to visit this place again unless I could carry Mr. Russell with me and witness his first interview with the domain."

From a letter by JOHN FORBES, President of the Michigan Central Railroad. 1847.

Benzonia

"Growing up in Benzonia was just a bit like growing up with the Twelve Apostles for next-door neighbors."

BRUCE CATTON. *Waiting for the Morning Train.* 1972. The town was founded by a Congregational minister who intended to establish a "Christian Colony & Institution of Learning." As Mr. Catton attests, the town lived up to the religious ideals well into the 20th century.

"The name of this town was Benzonia, and when we tried to tell strangers about it we usually had trouble because most peo-ple refused to believe there was any such word."

BRUCE CATTON. *Waiting for the Morning Train.* 1972.

"... a town so small that the car wash has been designated as a landmark."

SONNY ELIOT. *Michigan Living.* September 1988.

Big Bay

"... a little village with a big name. ..."

KENNETH S. LOWE. *Motor News.* May 1963.

"Big Bay is the only place I know with more places to stay than there are things to do."

RICK SYLVAIN. *Detroit Free Press.* June 28, 1992.

Birmingham

"Birmingham started expanding after the last big war as the waiting room for Grosse Pointe, a place where new money was left to mellow and season in brick splitlevels before moving into the great Prohibition-era mausoleums on Lake Shore Drive."

LOREN ESTLEMAN. *Silent Thunder.* 1989.

"Michigan's most fashion-conscious, glitziest downtown."

MARY and DON HUNT. *Hunt's Highlights of Michigan.* 1991.

Bloomfield Hills

"Five square miles of money."

LAURIE BENNETT. *Detroit Free Press Magazine.* January 31, 1993.

Boyne City

"Boyne City is an enterprising little town whose interests are mostly lumber. It does not command the special attention of visitors. ..."

JAMES GALE INGLIS. *Northen Michigan Handbook for Travelers.* 1898.

Cadillac

"... the nearest thing to Sodom and Gomorah since the original."

Detroit News. April 1882.

Calumet

See also *Architecture* (Calumet Opera House) and *Mining*

• Calumet was founded as a company town by the Calumet and Hecla Co.

"... the metropolis of Copperdom."

ALFRED NICHOLS, describing the city during the 1860s. *More Copper Country Tales.* 1968.

"The company owned everything: the mines, the school, the library, the stores, the hospital, the coal supply, the water pumps, the garbage wagons, the church and the hymnbooks in the church. It owned the houses. It owned the red paint that added the identical finishing touch to every identical house. It owned the toilets."

ROBERT CONOT, describing the city during the 1870s. *American Odyssey.* 1974.

"On Saturday evening the streets of Red Jacket have no parallel in the entire upper peninsula, so densely crowded are they with people so general of race and national-ity, that for its size, the place is undoubtedly the most cosmopolitan town in America."

Marquette Daily Mining Journal. 1897. Red Jacket was one of several settlements that made up Calumet.

"... a curious settlement, which is neither a town nor a city nor a village, and is perhaps the richest community of its size in the world. ... It is not incorporated, it has no organized form of government ... but it is a perfect example of a town, complete, with all public institutions."

WILLIAM ELEORY CURTIS, journalist. 1899.

"The Calumet area is sopped in history and each year, thousands of visitors poke their noses into corners of yesterdays. ..."

DAVID MACFRIMODIG. *Keweenaw Character.* 1990.

Charlevoix

"Numerous writers have painted pen pictures of the village of Charlevoix, some very successfully, but none have been able to embody in the sketch a charm that the subject does not possess."

Traverse Region, Historical & Descriptive. 1884.

"Nothing can exceed the almost fairy-tale beauty of this exquisite harbor. ..."

JAMES GALE INGLIS. *Northern Michigan Handbook for Travelers.* 1898.

"Charlevoix is reputed the most exclusive of Lake Michigan resorts: it calls itself 'the Newport of the West.' "

WEBB WALDRON. *We Explore the Great Lakes.* 1923.

"At times, there is nothing to do in Charlevoix but sit on a park bench, eat fudge and watch the drawbridge go up and down. And that is much of the beauty of Charlevoix. ..."

BILL CARROLL. *Michigan Living*. October 1977.

Charlotte

"Charlotte shows some improvement. I notice a new white stripe in the center of the trunk line on Lawrence Avenue. Frank Higby is washing his house, and I note several new haircuts, including my own. Outside of that, little change."

EMERSON BAYLESS, a Charlotte native, in a letter to a friend in the Armed Forces. August 1944.

Cheboygan

"... Cheboygan is especially adapted to the overworked professional or business man in search of some locality where he may recuperate his vital powers, and after remaining here for even a short time, he goes back to his business with renewed zest and vigor, amply repaying him for the trouble he may have taken to obtain them."

DOCTOR A. M. GEROW, of Cheboygan, who in 1876 also thought his hometown's climate could cure consumption, hay fever, asthma, dyspepsia, bowel complaints and general debility.

Chelsea

"No more tripping the light fantastic at Chelsea this season. At the last dance there the breath of the girls was so strong that many of the boys felt quamish and now declare they will not be caught in such a snap again. It is said there is but one girl in Chelsea who owns a tooth brush and she combs her eyebrows with it."

Unknown Grass Lake area newspaper. December 20, 1890.

Colon

"Colon is a village of about 1,000 or so, and could pass for a life-size set of 'Our Town.'"

NEELY TUCKER. *Detroit Free Press Magazine*. April 19, 1992.

Copper Harbor

See also *Military Forts* (Fort Wilkins) and *Mining*

"The country is bleak, barren and savage, without any signs of cultivation or civilization except the appearance of bedbugs and whiskey; rats and cockroaches have not yet come up, but are expected. ... It is a land of dirty shirts and long beards."

Unknown early resident of the copper boom town. 1840.

"Among dealers, arithmetic is not considered a necessary accomplishment, or a Christian virtue."

Unknown early resident of the copper boom town. 1840.

"The wilderness was at Copper Harbor's back and, in the winter, at its throat."

JOHN MARTIN, describing the area during the 1840s. *Call It North Country*. 1971.

"It is undoubtedly a bleak point."

LT. COLONEL HENRY WHITING. April 1844.

"... a miserable, barren place."

BRIG. GENERAL BRADY on reaching Copper Harbor in 1844.

"Card playing, the use of the 'flowing bowl,' and some good fighting with fist and pistol, were the social amusements of this conglomerate community. ... It was a common saying that there was no Sunday west of the Sault."

JOHN HARRIS FORSTER, describing the area in 1846. "Early Settlement of the Copper Region of Lake Michigan," *Michigan Pioneer Collection, Vol. VII.*

"Copper Harbor, once so busy and attractive, is now a deserted village."

JOHN HARRIS FORSTER, describing the community in 1888. "Early Settlement of the Copper Harbor Region of Lake Michigan," *Michigan Pioneer Collection, Vol. VII.*

"Copper Harbor is a quiet, remote village visited mainly for the beauty of its surrounding bluffs and shoreline."

EDWIN WAY TEALE. *Journey Into Summer.* 1969.

Cross Village

"It is simple justice to the tourist to inform him that no tour in this region is complete without a visit to the quaint and historic little town of Cross Village."

J. G. INGLIS. *Northern Michigan Handbook for Travelers.* 1898.

Dearborn

"... a tight white island of Poles, Syrians, and Italians. ... The 1970 census found 13 Negroes in Dearborn, but their location is a well-kept secret."

NEAL PEIRCE. *The Megastates of America.* 1972.

DeTour

"DeTour is a village of 600 weathered

persons."

WALTER HAVINGHURST. *Land of Promise.* 1946.

"DeTour, Michigan, at the mouth of the twisting and inspiringly scenic St. Mary's River, is 350 miles, by road, from Detroit, Michigan — but there are 3,000 miles of difference between the two towns!"

JOHN T. NEVILL. *Wanderings: Sketches of Northern Michigan Yesterday and Today.* 1955.

"... the ghastly truth seems to be that DeTour, once a bustling operating base for both lumberman and fisherman, may have more sunken vessels per lineal foot of waterfront than any other port on the Great Lakes. ..."

JOHN T. NEVILL. *Wandering: Sketches of Northern Michigan Yesterday and Today.* 1955.

Detroit

See also *Architecture* (Belle Isle Aquarium, Detroit Windsor Tunnel, Fisher Building, Fox Theater, Hudsons, and Renaissance Center), *Automobiles, Bridges* (Ambassador), *Islands* (Belle Isle) and *Rivers* (Detroit River)

"The ground here is very good for building eventually a large town."

ALFONSO TONTI, commandant of Detroit from 1704 to 1706.

"Detroit was founded because an ancient King of France wore a beaver hat."

MALCOLM BINGAY. *Detroit Is My Own Home Town.* 1946.

"... all the people here are generally poor wretches, and consist of three or four hundred French families, a lazy, idle people, depending chiefly on the savages for their subsistence. ..."

GEORGE CROGHAN. 1765

"It is something wonderful here and pleasant if anyone is found who shows a desire for God's word, for the place here is like Sodom, where all sins are committed."

Observation of a Moravian minister on visiting Detroit. 1782.

"... this is at present the most miserable place in all Canada: you will not find a family for fifty miles but three parts of them are languishing under the Fever Ague, or otherwise a violent bilious fever which has carried off numbers. ... I do not mean to stay one day longer in the place than the expiration of my agreement, for I never detested any place so much."

JOHN ASKWITH, a clerk in Detroit, in a letter to Montreal on November 7, 1793.

"The town itself is a crowded mass of frame or wooden buildings, generally from one to two and a half stories high, many of them well furnished, and inhabited by people of almost all nations. ... The streets are so narrow as scarcely to admit carriages to pass each other."

GENERAL ANTHONY WAYNE. 1796.

"The inhabitants of this place have lived for many years past in a state of licentious freedom, nor can they now bear to be checked. Nothing but a more severe law can bring them to order."

PATRICK MCNIFF, lamenting the lack of orderly government or civil laws in the city. 1799.

"For the space of thirty days and thirty nights he viewed the diurnal evolution of the planets, visible and invisible, and calculated the course and rapidity of the blazing meteors. To his profound observings of the heavenly regions the world is indebted for the discovery of the streets, alleys, circles, angles, and squares of this magnificent city."

Self-appointed social critic and cynic JOHN GENTLE's tongue-in-cheek remarks on the work of Judge Woodward's imported surveyor who laid out the street plan for Detroit. 1800s.

"... the modern Boshorus."

JUDGE AUGUSTUS WOODWARD, describing the city in 1805. *Michigan Pioneer Collection, Vol. XII.*

"Nature has destined the city of Detroit to be a great interior emporium, equal, if not superior, to any other on the surface of the terraqueous globe."

JUDGE AUGUSTUS WOODWARD. 1818.

"There is no place in the world more healthy than Detroit."

ESTIVICK EVANS. *A Predestrious Tour of Four Thousand Miles, Through the Western States and Territories, During the Winter and Spring of 1818.*

"In Detroit there is much good society; and hospitality is a conspicious trait in the character of the people. ... In time, this city will become conspicious for its literature, and for the propriety of its customs and manners."

ESTIVICK EVANS. *A Predestrious Tour of Four Thousand Miles, Through the Western States and Territories, During the Winter and Spring of 1818.*

"Detroit, politically and comercially, is separated by an expanse of water, and by an uncultivated waste, from the other parts of the United States, and remains, together with the little community of its environs, an isolated moral mass, having few sympathies in common, and but a slight tie of interest to unite it to the sovereignty of which it forms a part."

WILLIAM DARBY. *A Tour From the City of New York, to Detroit, in the Michigan Territory.* 1819.

"It is truly a matter of astonishment that many of the citizens of Detroit, who have resided here for forty years and upwards, should be profoundly ignorant of the country twenty miles back from the river."

Detroit Gazette. September 1, 1820.

"I should think from appearances that this might be a healthy place and a place of Considerable business tho like every other place along the Lake there is to much compition for the binifit of the mercantile part of the community."

SALMON KEENEY. An entry in his diary of a trip to Michigan in 1827.

"I have seen a plot of this city. I wish for the sake of its designer, towards whom, personally, I entertain the kindest feelings, that it had never been conceived by him. It looks pretty on paper, but is fanciful; and resembles one of those octagonal spider webs which you have seen in a dewy morning, with a centre, you know, and lines leading out to points around the circumference, and fastened to spires of grass. The citizens of Detroit would do well, in my opinion, and their posterity would thank them for it, were they to reduce the network of that plan to something practical and regular."

THOMAS L. MCKENNEY. *Sketches of a Tour of the Lakes.* 1827.

"Detroit has long been regarded as the limit of civilization towards the north-west — and to tell truth, there is even yet little of the character of civilization beyond."

C. COLTON. *Tour of the American Lakes.* 1830.

"I went up Jefferson Avenue, found some brick buildings, barber poles, wooden clocks or large watches, big hats and boots,

a brass ball, etc. I returned to the hotel satisfied that Detroit was actually a city, for the things I had seen were, in my mind, sufficient to make it one."

An unknown traveler to Detroit in 1834.

"There is not a paved street in it, or even a foot-path for a pedestrian. In winter, in rainy weather you are up to your knees in mud; in summer, invisible in dust; indeed, until lately there was not a practical road for thirty miles around Detroit."

From the diary of CAPTAIN MARRYAT, a popular British novelist of the early 1800s.

"The plan of the city is rather uncouth and laboured, with much mathematical ingenuity, better suited, it is acknowledged, to flatter the fancy than to promote practical utility."

JOHN T. BLOIS. *Gazetteer of the State of Michigan.* 1838.

"... no poor man could become Governor as the salary ($1,500) would not support him in the gay city, while it was sufficient to enable the poor but ambitious man to live in the simplicity of the interior villages."

A popular argument in the 1840s for moving the capital of Michigan from Detroit.

"You must lock your state-rooms at night for Detroit is full of thieves."

Advice to William Cullen Bryant from a ship's employee when Bryant stayed the night in Detroit. From a letter by Bryant on July 24, 1846.

"... the site was formed by nature for prosperity."

FRANCIS PARKMAN. *The Conspiracy of Pontiac.* 1851.

"Will there ever be any safety to property or life in Detroit? Probably not."

Detroit Advertizer. November 23, 1854.

"Tampa of the North."

A common nickname for Detroit in the 1880s, when the city's single most important product was tobacco, which included the production of 40 million cigars annually.

"A commonplace and very communistic-looking city — but, I suppose, a fair type of many a city in the West. The dull flatness of the country in which the city lies — the oppressive lack of interest and variety in the city itself — the sameness of the people; here are three phenomena to be set down as closely connected."

CHARLES W. ELIOT, President of Harvard University. 1883.

"The people of Detroit perhaps inherit the pleasure-loving characteristics of their French ancestors, or at least they do not seem to have their minds exclusively concentrated on the struggle after the almighty dollar."

CAPTAIN WILLARD GLAZIER. 1883.

"In the 1890s, Detroit was a quiet, tree-shaded city, unobtrusively going about its business of brewing beer and making carriages and stoves."

ALAN CLIVE. *State of War: Michigan in World War II.* 1979.

"Cradled in romance, nurtured in war, and trained in the school of conservatism, the city now glories in her position as the most attractive and most substational of all the cities whose traditions reach back to the days of the 'Grand Monarch.' "

SILAS FARMER. *History of Detroit and Wayne County and Early Michigan.* 1890.

"... one of the most healthy cities in the world."

SILAS FARMER. *History of Detroit and Wayne County and Early Michigan.* 1890.

"The first horseless carriage seen in this city was out on the streets last night. The apparatus seems to work all right, and it went at the rate of five or six miles an hour at an even rate of speed."

Detroit Free Press. March 7, 1896. The horseless carriage was designed and built by Charles Brady King.

"Detroit, where life is worth living."

Detroit Board of Commerce promotional slogan. 1890s.

"Perhaps no city on the Great Lakes is so intimately associated with the history of the Great Lakes as Detroit."

JOHN MANSFIELD. *History of the Great Lakes*. 1899.

"We hope to make Detroit as prominent a manufacturing town for automobiles as it is for stoves."

HENRY B. JOY, one of the founders of the Packard Motor Car Company. 1903.

"You can stand in a square of Detroit and the entire automobile business of the world will pass by, and you won't have to stand there very long, either."

HUGH CHALMERS, President of the Detroit Chalmers Motor Co. 1910.

"The favorite sport of the natives is seeing who can drive the fastest and furthest. The speed record is held jointly by several hundred thousand automobile owners, who have went 60 miles per hr. past a standing still st. car."

RING LARDNER. 1915.

"God, you've got a job on your hands in Detroit."

BILLY SUNDAY, famed evangelist during his month-long revival in Detroit in 1916.

"Automobiles are everywhere — automobiles in solid ranks along the curbs, automobiles rushing up and down in unbroken streams. Automobiles! Automobiles! Such is Detroit."

WEBB WALDRON. *The Century Magazine.* May 20, 1920.

"... Detroit has the worst (housing) situation of any city in America.

Mayor Cousins ... tells me he is in favor of building a wall around Detroit and keeping people out for six months, or, at least, of strongly advising people to stay away."

WEBB WALDRON. *The Century Magazine.* May 20, 1920.

"It is not surprising to find more automobiles per square foot in Detroit than in any other American city, but I was surprised to find automobile-driving more reckless here than anywhere else in my experience. It is evidently too much to expect that a city should both produce the motorcar and evolve ideas for its control."

WEBB WALDRON. *We Explore the Great Lakes.* 1923.

"... notwithstanding so large an industrial population, Detroit may fairly be described as a slumless city."

National Geographic. March 1928.

"Everywhere the traffic problem is seen in an endless procession of motorcars and parking spaces, where these cars are ranged as thickly as peas in a pod."

National Geographic. March 1928.

"It was absolutely impossible to get a drink in Detroit unless you walked at least ten feet and told a busy bartender what you wanted in a voice loud enough for him to hear you above the uproar."

Detroit journalist MALCOLM BINGAY, on Detroit during Prohibition.

"Detroit today is the wettest and widest open town in the country and has the largest per capita consumption of liquor of all the cities in the United States — New York included."

Plain Talk Magazine. 1930.

"I can say without reservation that Detroit is the wettest city I have ever been assigned to."

A. B. STROUP, Deputy Administrator of Prohibition Enforcement in Detroit. 1930.

"Detroit is a city on wheels. I would go so far as to say of Detroit that even its buildings somehow give the impression of being parked rather than rooted in the ground."

R. I. DEFFUS. *Detroit Free Press.* May 10, 1931.

"It is truly a world capital as any city on earth, more fascinating to the outsider than New York, more influential than Washington, or even Hollywood. Paris dictates a season's silhouette, but Detroit manufactures a pattern of life, bolder than Moscow in transforming human habits and communizing the output of the machine."

ANNE O'HARE McCORMICK. *New York Times.* November 11, 1934.

"Detroit was a model of racial segregation. Blacks were herded into a thirty block ghetto called Paradise Valley, and the Detroit Housing Commission and fifty 'neighborhood improvement associations' aided by the Ku Klux Klan, kept them there."

BRUCE RUBENSTEIN and LAWRENCE ZIEWACZ, characterizing the city during the 1940s. *Michigan: A History of the Great Lakes State.* 1981.

"(Detroit), where they stand in line for a glass of beer, ... where more dames wear slacks than in Hollywood, ... where it takes the reserves to get a vandal out of a theater, where the sidewalk madonnas get too much opposition from home talent, ... and where everybody has two sawbucks to rub against each other. Detroit, the hottest town in America."

Daily Variety. October 1943.

"Detroit has always been a sports minded community."

GEORGE W. STARK. *City of Destiny.* 1943.

"Detroit, Workshop to the World, resourceful, energetic, blatant."

HARLAN HATCHER. *The Great Lakes.* 1944.

"Detroit is usually hot and sticky in the summer, and in the winter the snow in the streets is like a dirty, worn-out blanket. Like other big cities it is best in the fall. ..."

KENNETH MILLAR. *The Dark Tunnel.* 1944.

"Detroit has little imposing about it except the factories, which are more imposing than almost anything else could be."

GRAHAM HUTTON. *Midwest at Noon.* 1946.

"Though founded two and a half centuries ago, Detroit still has the feeling of a frontier town."

WALTER HAVINGHURST. *Land of Promise.* 1946.

"I would say that Detroit was the most beautiful city of my trip. Except for a certain number of large buildings in the center, Detroit is casual, improvised, like an encampment: a conglomeration of worn out wooden houses, stores, warehouses, on the vast outlying districts some roadside lodgings called motels, of which there are hundreds of thousands in America. In all this confusion there are great gashes everywhere which recall our cities after bombardment."

Italain journalist GUIDO PIOVENE. 1952.

"... a city where repetition and monotony had been elevated to an art form."

BILL MORRIS. *Motor City.* 1954.

"Detroit may have a symphony and an art museum. But I never heard of anybody flying there to go to the opera. How can you have a romance with this city?"

A San Francisco travel writer responding to a survey sent to travel writers asking for their impressions of Detroit. *Motor News.* March 1963.

"... even many Detroit natives refuse to believe anyone in his right mind would come to see Detroit."

LEM BARNES. *Motor News.* May 1963.

"Equally important, the main problem of Detroit in this day and age seems to be what to do with a motorcar when it is not motoring."

SIR MILES THOMAS of Great Britain, on Detroit's parking problem. 1966.

"The tragedy was not that so much of the city was burned, but so little."

An unnamed aide of Mayor Cavanagh, after the 1967 Detroit riot.

TONY SPINA / DETROIT FREE PRESS

"It looked like the city had been bombed on the west side and there was an area two-and-a-half miles by three-and-a-half miles with major fires, with entire blocks in flames."

GOVERNOR GEORGE ROMNEY, after flying over Detroit during the 1967 riot.

"Detroit has always been thought of as a vibrant, can-do place. If you want to get something done, take this marvelous collection of technical people this city has ... Take the people and point them. The problem is to point them."

ROBERT HASTINGS, architect. 1970s.

"... grayness and the grit, the dirty
funky, hardheavy city, home of cheese-
    cake
hands and the baddest right hook you've
    ever seen."

b. p. FLANIGAN. *Freeway Series / 1.* 1970s.

"Detroit is the city of problems. If they exist, we've probably got them. We may not have them exclusively, that's for sure. But we probably had them first."

LAWRENCE M. CARINO, Chairman of the Greater Detroit Chamber of Commerce. 1972.

"Anybody who lives in Detroit lives the blues sometimes, if not all the time."

PAT HALLEY, reporter for the *Fifth Estate*. 1973.

"What most people know about Detroit is that it is big, it is the Motor City, it is industrial and there is no reason to go there."

OUTDOOR WORLD. *The Great Lakes: North America's Inland Sea.* 1974. The book goes on to prove that the above quote is a widely held misconception.

"I issue a warning now to all dope pushers, ripoff artists, and muggers. It is time to leave Detroit. Hit the road."

Detroit Mayor COLEMAN YOUNG. 1974.

"Of all cities, Detroit is the sum of our achievements and challenges, a frontier

outpost that became the most industrial-
ized and unionized city in the world."

The jacket blurb from *American Odyssey* by ROBERT
CONOT. 1974.

"Detroit is the heart of American industry, and by the beat of that heart much of
America's economic health is measured."

ROBERT CONOT. *American Odyssey.* 1974.

"We almost lost Detroit."

An anonymous engineer at the Enrico Fermi atomic
reactor near Monroe, reflecting (in 1975) on the possible consequences when the reactor suddenly suffered
a near melt-down on October 5, 1966.

"In grade school we studied all that.
Founded by Antoine de la Mothe Cadillac
in seventeen-whatever. But you know it's a
lie. Henry Ford founded Detroit in the
twenties and everything before that is
invented."

MARGE PIERCY. *The High Cost of Living.* 1978.

"After automobiles and murders, Detroit
is most famous for its riverfront ethnic fes-
tivals. ..."

LOREN ESTLEMAN. *The Midnight Man.* 1982.

"Windsor is just Detroit after the maid's
been in."

LOREN ESTLEMAN. *The Glass Highway.* 1983.

"Ceaseless motion, the pulse of the city.
    The beat. The beat.
A place of romance, the quintessential
    America city."

JOYCE CAROL OATES. "Visions of Detroit." *Michigan
Quarterly Review.* 1986.

"When it's February in Detroit it's been
winter forever."

LOREN ESTLEMAN. *Lady Yesterday.* 1987.

"When the history of the twentieth century is written, one of the bright highlights
may well be this interracial cooperation,
which oversaw the successful transition of
a major American city to black control."

MARTHA BIGELOW. "Michigan: A State in the
Vanguard." *Heartland.* 1988.

"This city is just one big ghetto, all the
way out to Eight Mile Road."

Detroit Police Chief WILLIAM HART. 1988.

"The history of guns is the history of
Detroit, from the day Cadillac's men daz-
zled the local indians with the rattle and
flame of the muskets to last Friday, when a
sixteen-year-old boy shot down another boy
... for looking at him wrong."

LOREN ESTLEMAN. *Silent Thunder.* 1989.

"When I was growing up, Detroit made
one promise to its young people — a good
job. A place on the line at GM, Ford or
Chrysler was a part of our birthright, a
legacy to the city's children. And then in
the early seventies that legacy was withdrawn."

ZE'EV CHAFETS. *Devils Night and Other True Tales of
Detroit.* 1990.

"In Detroit, Christianity — specifically
black Protestant fundamentalism —
approaches the status of state doctrine."

ZE'EV CHAFETS. *Devils Night and Other True Tales of
Detroit.* 1990.

"America's first Third World City."

ZE'EV CHAFETS. *Devils Night and Other True Tales of Detroit*. 1990.

"When they were stumped in ancient Greece, they went to the oracle of Delphi. At Lourdes they take the waters, and I suppose in Akron they go down and watch tires being made. In Detroit, where we put the world on wheels or did anyway until the Japanese and Yugoslavs and the Brits rolled in, when our brains slip into neutral we lay rubber on the road and hit the gas."

LOREN ESTLEMAN. *Sweet Women Lie*. 1990.

"Detroit — where the weak are killed and eaten."

Slogans on T-shirts sold in Detroit's Greek town. 1991.

"... Detroit is really the last great Southern town. Here amid the industrial decay of the city which first offered well-paid work for blacks, back around the time of the First World War, is where Voodoo and deep south persist, not in the shopping malls of the New South."

JOHN WILLIAMS. *Into the Badlands: Travels Through Urban America*. 1991.

"... you have to understand Detroit — the city of the People Mover, the People's Bank, the People Community this or that. No social barriers of even borders allowed. There's barely enough rules to prevent chaos, and sometimes they fail. Anyone with the price of admission can go anywhere and be as big a pain in the ass as they want and no one is going to stop them, because if they do lawsuits for discrimination are as predictable as their lawyer's ethics."

PAUL LINDSEY. *Witness for the Truth*. 1992.

"... one of the most violent and drug-ridden cities in America."

DORON P. LEVIN. *New York Times*. March 23, 1993.

"... it's a little odd to hear someone from Detroit calling Flint names. I mean, if Flint's the belt buckle of the Rust Belt, what's that make Detroit? The zipper?"

ANDREW HELLER. *Flint Journal*. March 7, 1993. The columnist was taking exception to a March 1, 1993 article in the *Detroit Free Press* that called Flint the "out-of-work buckle of the rust belt."

Eagle Harbor

"... one of the most completely beautiful villages I ever expect to see."

BRUCE CATTON. *Holiday Magazine*. August 1957.

Eagle River

"... has a fine beach for a harbor, a boarding-house, a sawmill, and a store, where drinking is the principal business transacted."

CHARLES LANMAN. *A Summer in the Wilderness*. 1847.

"Eagle river is an inconsiderable stream, except where at it's mouth, emptying into Lake Superior about twenty-five miles west of Copper Harbor. The small town at the mouth bears the same name. The site is an immense sand-bank, and has no attractiveness."

REV. JOHN H. PITEZEL, describing the town in 1848. *Lights and Shades of Missionary Life*. 1859.

East Detroit

"East Detroit is an angry child, connected to the mother city by a steel umbilical cord and despising every inch of it. ... it's a landlocked community that yearns to be an island and lacks only the business, industry, self-awareness and courage to succeed."

LOREN ESTLEMAN. *Sweet Women Lie.* 1990.

Eaton Rapids

"It is the finest little village in the known world. ..."

Future Michigan Governor AUSTIN BLAIR's first impression of the small frontier settlement. 1842.

"The Saratoga of the West."

Michigan Historical Marker. Eaton Rapids became a very popular health resort in the late 1880s after mineral water was discovered in the area. Thousands came to drink and bathe in the city's waters. The last bath closed in 1962.

Ecorse

"... to have seen Ecorse in its palmy days is an unforgettable experience, for no gold camp of the old West presented a more glamorous spectacle. It was a perpetual carnival of drinking, gambling and assorted vices."

Journalist F. L. SMITH JR., recalling the city during Prohibition.

"... Michigan's 'Barbary Coast.' "

LARRY ENGELMANN, describing the city during the 1930s. *Intemperance: The Lost War Against Liquor.* 1979.

Elmira

"Elmira is a town consisting of a single house in the woods. ..."

A. JUDD NORTHRUP. *Camps and Tramps in the Adirondacks and Grayling Fishing in Northern Michigan.* 1880.

Engadine

"A charming little village where harsh memories are as scarce as suggestion boxes in the Kremlin."

SONNY ELIOT. *Michigan Living.* September 1988.

Escanaba

"... mistress of the iron trade of both hemispheres."

WALTER NURSEY. *The City of Escanaba.* 1890. In 1890 Escanaba shipped four million tons of iron ore on some 3,000 ships.

"Escanaba is one of those places where the business section is five miles from the railroad station — or so, in those scaggely discouraged streets, it seemed. The main street, which I reached at last, was a wide, desolate thoroughfare ending at the beach."

WEBB WALDRON. *We Explore the Great Lakes.* 1923.

"... the Riviera of the North."

JEAN R. KOMAIKO, et al. *Around Lake Michigan.* 1980.

Ferrysburg

"Saratoga of the Middle West."

Great Lakes Waterway Guide. 1960.

Flint

"This is the town where they sleep them so thick that their feet hang out the window."

JOHN IHLDER. *The Survey.* September 2, 1916.

"... Flint is rich: that is, it feels rich, it talks rich and it has a rich income."

JOHN IHLDER. *The Survey.* September 2, 1916

"It was a poor man who could not make money in Flint."

EDMUND G. LOVE, describing the city during the 1920s. *Hanging On: Or How to Get Through a Depression and Enjoy Life.* 1987.

"The city of Flint is one of the industrial wonders of our modern civilization."

WILLARD M. BRYANT. *Michigan History Magazine.* July/October 1921.

"... the greatest little city in the world."

BILLY DURANT, founder of General Motors. 1930s.

"Automobile manufacture has made Flint a rich city."

Michigan: A Guide to the Wolverine State. 1941.

"This City of Flint is a place where nearly everyone came from somewhere else, and many a man rates himself a simon-pure old timer because he reached here around 1925."

ARTHUR POUND, in a speech given before the Historical Society of Michigan at Flint in 1955.

"... the epitome of the blue-collar lunch-bucket city and General Motors town par excellence."

NEAL PEIRCE. *The Megastates of America.* 1972

"No one can understand ennui, dullness, until he has spent three days sitting on a front porch in Flint."

RAYMOND SOKOLOV. *Native Intelligence.* 1975.

"Waiting is the worst thing in the world, especially waiting in Flint. This little city is like one big front porch with a view of a 24-hour traffic jam."

RAYMOND SOKOLOV. *Native Intelligence.* 1975.

"Flint is still a company town, and General Motors is the company."

ROGER L. ROSENTRETER. *Michigan History Magazine.* May/June 1982.

"... a hard, dreary town, a working-man's town of white men and black men who trace their roots to the pre-World War II South and earned, on the average, the highest industrial wages in the United States."

RICHARD POWERS. *American Journey.* 1982.

"It's been said that in economic terms when America sneezes, Detroit gets pneumonia. If that's true, then Flint must go into the intensive care unit."

GEORGE CANTOR. *Michigan Living.* August 1986.

"We have more Coney Island restaurants per square mile than any other city, but we also have an elaborate cultural center."

Flint Mayor MATTHEW S. COLLIER. *Michigan Living.* May 1990. The mayor's reply when asked why his city was outstanding.

"A town where every infant twirls a set of channel locks in place of a rattle. A town whose collective bowling average is four times higher than the IQ of its inhabitants.

A town that genuflects in front of used car lots ... where having a car up on blocks anywhere on your property bestows upon you a privileged sense of royalty."

BEN HAMPER. *Rivethead.* 1991.

"Woebegon Flint, the crime-invested, out-of-work buckle of the Rust Belt."

LORI MONTGOMERY. *Detroit Free Press.* March 1, 1993.

Frankenmuth

See also *Tourism* (Bronners)

"Certainly, the 15 German settlers who conquered the thick virgin forests here in 1845 had something more noble than chicken wings on their minds."

SHERYL JAMES. *Detroit Free Press Magazine.* November 15, 1992.

Bavarian Inn

TOM POWERS

Zehnders

"No one in Germany can possibly picture to himself an American farm. The sight is so wretched and sad that people who come with great expectations into this promised land break out in tears and find it difficult to console themselves. ... The most miserable village in Germany has palaces by comparison."

A Frankenmuth colonist of 1846, in a letter home to Germany.

"After we ... had traveled 12 miles, the guide turned to the left and we rejoiced that we had only four miles to Frankenmuth. But then we really entered the wilderness. Of a road nothing more was

to be seen. Cart and attendants sought a way between trees and brushwood as best they could. ... Then suddenly the guide stopped before a log house in the midst of the thick brush and cried: Here we are!"

GEORGE A. RANZENBERGER, recalling his arrival in Frankenmuth in 1846.

"Boston named baked beans, the Creoles named their shrimp dish, Kansas City its beef, but Frankenmuth named its chicken dinners and made that name known across the nation."

HERMAN F. ZEHNDER. *Teach My People the Truth.* 1970.

"... Frankenmuth today is in the great American tradition of too much of everything."

MARY and DON HUNT. *Hunt's Highlights of Michigan.* 1991.

"Chickenmuth."

Grandchildren telling their grandfather where they wanted to go for dinner. 1992.

"Frankenmuth rises unexpectedly from cow pastures, a perfect vision of a tourist's perfect vision of Bavaria. It has the sunny disposition and squeaky cleanliness of the Magic Kingdom, every detail has been considered, refined, perfected."

SHERYL JAMES. *Detroit Free Press Magazine.* November 15, 1992.

Franklin

"Franklin is a little country village containing 100 inhabitants. I do not believe it is any more worthy of notice than other rural villages which beautify the countryside in almost every direction."

Pontiac Gazette. July 12, 1855.

Freidberger

"... may be the worst town name in the nation."

WILLIAM LEAST HEAT MOON. *Blue Highways.* 1982

Gaines

"There is one gas station, a post office, a tavern, a party store and one grocery still in the town. The depot is deserted, the last train stopped in 1958. Gaines did not ever have a newspaper, or library and no one seems to care. Life in Gaines is still far different from life in cities and suburbs a short freeway drive away. Gaines — a quiet, little town, on the way to somewhere."

M. ZDUNIC. "Early Development of the Gaines Area," in *A Wind Gone Down: Out of the Wilderness.* Michigan, Department of History. 1978.

Gay

"The year-round population of Gay has plummeted from a peak of more than 1,200 to about 50 loyal residents, who are occasionally outnumbered by the herd of deer they feed throughout the winter."

DAVID MacFRIMODIG. *Keweenaw Character.* 1990.

"What do I do? Drink beer. Is there something else to do?"

One of the residents of the tiny Keweenaw Peninsula village. *Detroit Free Press.* June 28, 1992.

Glennie

"Nearly everyone's been there, has heard about it, knows someone there, or plans on going there sometime."

HAZEL GIRARD. *Blow for Blatten's Crossing.* 1979.

Grand Haven

"For twenty long tedious, dreary winters, we have been shut up in solitary confinement for no fault of ours that we know of, for if you take our word for it, we are a most virtuous, sober, religious people as you can find on this continent. At all events here we were winter after winter like bears in hibernations, as the story goes, sucking our paw."

Grand Haven News. December 22, 1858. An editorial celebrating the coming of the railroad to Grand Haven.

"The Riviera of the North."

Great Lakes Waterway Guide. 1960.

"Caution — friendly area ahead."

Billboard just outside of Grand Haven during the 1960s.

Grand Marais

"It is a quiet little backside-of-nowhere sort of place, huddled among sand hills at the end of a twenty-five mile spur road out of Seney, its weatherbeaten buildings carrying the air of proud but desperate poverty that is called 'picturesque' by those who have never had to endure it."

WILLIAM ASHWORTH. *The Late Great Lakes*. 1987.

"A town so petite that as one writer was inspired to comment, 'you can drive through in six heartbeats.' "

DORIS SCHARFENBERG. *Long Blue Edge of Summer*. 1992.

"... no one is likely to visit Grand Marais on the way to somewhere else."

ROBERT CROSS. *Chicago Tribune Magazine*. August 30, 1992.

Grand Rapids

"... a hundred miles from nowhere."

ABEL DREW and WAIT FARR, two settlers from Vermont, writing home about the new town of Grand Rapids. 1830s.

"The surrounding country is one of the most beautiful and fertile imaginable, and its rise to wealth and populousness must be a mere question of time."

HENRY SCHOOLCRAFT. 1838.

"... it is a matter of comment by strangers who visit us that we have not outgrown the habits and peculiarities of the country village."

Mayor EDWIN F. UHL, in his inaugural address. 1890.

"... that city has for many years enjoyed a widespread popularity, good will and demand throughout the United States, and the words 'Grand Rapids furniture' have acquired in the trade a special significance."

The Seventh Circuit of Appeals in Chicago, rendering an opinion barring a Chicago furniture maker from using the name "Grand Rapids Furniture Co." 1942.

"... a city that had to be."

Z. Z. LYDENS. *The Story of Grand Rapids*. 1966.

"... once a placid city of white, blond-haired Republican conservatives who all seemed to have some sort of Van in front of their surnames."

NEAL PEIRCE. *The Great Lakes States of America*. 1980.

"Furniture manufacturers may have put Grand Rapids on the map but Gerald R. Ford added the pin."

JEAN SIMMONS. *Michigan Living*. April 1988.

Grayling

"If they ever succeed in putting large areas of this country on the market it will be done by selling the ozone and throwing in the land."

G. MASON FANNING. *Detroit News Tribune.* August 31, 1913.

"The town of Grayling was built on sawdust and named after a fish. But, man what a fish!"

HAZEN MILLER. *The Old Au Sable.* 1963.

"... a fishing and deer-hunting town gone to K-marts and Ben Franklin stores and chain restaurants."

LOREN ESTLEMAN. *Downriver.* 1979.

Grosse Pointe

"... Grosse Pointe can hold its head up with any place anywhere. ..."

GRAHAM HUTTON. *Midwest at Noon.* 1946.

"... a closed-in, compact strip of privilege and cool green shade ... dwelling place for la creme de la creme of Detroit's nuts-and-bolts society."

NEAL PEIRCE. *The Megastates of America.* 1972.

Hamtramck

"The wild west in the middle west."

Wayne County Prosecutor PAUL VOORHIES, when he called in the State Police to clean up the illegal gambling and vice flourishing in the city. 1924.

"The first qualification for public office in Hamtramck is a prison term."

A common saying of the 1940s because of the graft and corruption in the city's government.

"A ... Polish island inside Detroit."

Life Magazine. August 17, 1942.

"... when a candidate for Mayor in Hamtramck promised a clean up and was elected, it was discovered that he was thinking of the streets and alleys rather than blind-pigs and disorderly resorts."

New York Times. July 7, 1951.

"One of the most purely Polish neighborhoods west of Warsaw. ..."

BILL MORRIS, describing the city as it was in 1954. *Motor City.* 1992.

Harbor Beach

"People who argue that pretty towns and industry cannot live together should look at Harbor Beach."

WILLIAM LEAST HEAT MOON. *Blue Highways.* 1982.

Harbor Springs

"Though there wasn't the slightest resemblance between squalid little Harbor Springs ... to Naples or the Bay of Naples, our two village newspapers called Harbor Springs the 'Naples of the North.' "

U. P. HENDRICK, describing the city area during the 1870s. *Land of the Crooked Tree.* 1948.

Harper Woods

"Harper Woods is strictly for local residents who don't want a Detroit address. ... It has no history and no business section to speak of, just rows and rows of houses and a school or two and some trees to justify the second half of its name and more churches than you can shake a prayer book at."

LOREN ESTLEMAN. *Every Brilliant Eye.* 1986.

Harrison

"... the most motley gathering of lumberjacks, roustabouts and shady characters ever to be assembled in one place."

ROY L. DODGE, describing the town as it was in the 1880s. *Ticket to Hell: A Saga of Michigan's Bad Men.* 1975.

Hartford

"So far as I have been able to discover, the history of the town is as lacking in distinction as its name."

WILLIS F. DUNBAR. *How It Was in Hartford.* 1968.

Harvey

"... two blocks of boarded-over storefronts and depressed tourist trade. ..."

LOREN ESTLEMAN. *Downriver.* 1988.

Hastings

"We're like Mayberry with an attitude."

SHIRLEY MARSH, owner of Ritchie's Koffe Shop in Hastings, explaining why she thinks her town was listed in "The 100 Best Small Towns in America." 1993.

Hell

GARY W. BARFKNECHT

"The road to Hell is paved with asphalt. ..."

GARY BARFKNECHT. *Ultimate Michigan Adventures.* 1989.

Holland

"If we stopped just outside the small dwelling of Mr. Fairbanks, we were on all sides surrounded by virgin forest in which wildlife was almost undisturbed. ... Everything was still equally rough and wild; suited for nothing, you would think, but a habitation for the wild animals of the forest."

EGBERT FREDERKS, an early settler of Holland, recalling how the site looked in 1847.

"At midnight we landed at the foot of Fifth Street in what was called the City of Holland, really a dense forest of big trees — timber of all kinds. The air was full of malaria caused by the swamp, stagnant water and dirty waters of Black Lake — a place of sickness and death."

ENGBERTUS VAN DER VEEN, an early settler of Holland. 1848.

"There was nothing soft about the Dutch Puritans on the Michigan frontier. They were quite as capable of plucking out their own eye if it offended them as the English Puritans had been two centuries earlier."

ARNOLD MULDER, describing the area's residents of the late 1840s. *Americans From Holland.* 1947.

"... the Hollanders who settled in Michigan were so ignorant of the ways of forest life that they literally did not know how to cut down a tree."

ARNOLD MULDER, describing the area's residents of the 1840s. *Americans From Holland.* 1947.

Honor

"Except for the lack of stone fences and a steepled white-frame church, Honor could be a New England town transplanted in the Midwest. It is surrounded by similiar-looking hills ablaze with October frost fires. The famous Platte River purls along like a New Hampshire freshet. Reclusive artists live in its environs. And reticent homeown-ers and shopkeepers bear a wariness of the probing questions and the photographers flash, not at all unlike tight-jawed, redneck farmers of Maine."

TOM HUGGLER. *Midwest Meanders.* 1984.

Howell

"Howell was a town from the start with a grin on its continence, which never relaxed but continually flowed into guf-faws."

Judge JEROME W. TURNER, in an address before the Livingston County Historical Society, circa 1990.

Idlewild

• Idlewild was established shortly before World War I as a resort for African-Americans.

"When you stand in Idlewild and look around at Nature's beauty, breathe the

Houghton

"We have two seasons: winter's here and winter's coming."

"We have two seasons: winter and bad sledding."

"The four seasons are early winter, mid-winter, late winter, and next winter."

Classic jokes told by the citizens of Houghton about their long winters.

FLINT JOURNAL

Annual Snow Sculpturing Contest
Michigan Technological University (Houghton)

fresh air and note the freedom form preju-
dice, ostracism and hatred, you can feel
yourself truly an American citizen."

DR. THOMAS W. BURTON. 1920.

Imlay City

"... a small one-stop-sign town with an
ambitious name."

RONALD JAGER, describing how he viewed the city as
it was in the 1930s. *Eighty Acres.* 1990.

Interlochen

• The fine arts camp founded at the city of
Interlochen in 1927 is the most prestigious
and successful in the country.

"Suddenly each summer on the lake
shores of northern Michigan a living truth
is rekindled. I have felt its glow all the way
around the world, across the continents
and across borderlines that let down their
barriers only for those who know the uni-
versal password. ... Interlochen is a magic
word in the music world."

VAN CLIBURN. 1968.

"... the mother of all summer art camps."

JOHN GUINN. *Detroit Free Press.* September 6, 1992.

Ionia

"Ionia prides itself on the good order,
moral worth and respectability of the people. ... A few boys walk the street with a
cigar in their mouths; for it must not be
supposed that in a place as large as Ionia

all will know what belongs to a gentleman,
or that all boys have been well brought up."

FRANKLIN EVERETT. *Memorials of the Grand River
Valley.* 1878.

Iron Mountain

"The place was alive with men and full
of sin."

REV. W. G. PUDDLEFOOT, describing the area during
the 1860s. *The Minute Man on the Frontier.* 1895.

Jackson

"A more forbidding site for a village or
city than that chosen for Jackson could not
in all probability have been found in the
state of Michigan."

Reminiscences by an unnamed early settler of the
town. 1830s.

"My chapel was the bar-room of a log
tavern, with the bottles staring me in the
face. But they did not adulterate the truth,
though probably some of the congregation
who did not imbibe the spirit of the sermon
did imbibe the spirit of the bottles. ...
Jackson was a wild, rough, and very
unpromising place to build a town, and the
inhabitants were poor and many of them
very much dispirited, but they had no
alternative but to stay and shake it out.
Many of them shook most fearfully."

Recollections of a pioneer preacher, name unknown.
1831.

"... a place of bad water and smart yan-
kees."

FRANCIS LAMBIE of Ypsilanti recalling his brief move
to Jackson in 1846.

Kalamazoo

"Right now there is no better way of investing money than by buying government land in the best sections of Kalamazoo and letting it lie."

KARL NEIDHARD, a German traveler to Michigan in 1835.

"One great mass convention of men almost raving with land mania. Everybody was crazy for land, and felt rich and wanted to be crazier and richer still."

Pioneer historian GEORGE TORREY, remembering the rush for land around Kalamazoo in 1836.

"Neither Andalusian plains, nor enamelled islands in tropic seas would so gratify the scientific and curious visitor as the prospect of our wood-shaded and wood-begirt village."

Kalamazoo Gazette. 1838.

"... an unusually pretty village."

JAMES FENIMORE COOPER. *Oak Openings.* 1848

"Kalamazoo is one of the most attractive towns in Michigan, and, indeed, in the country. It is situated on a broad plateau, through which its beautiful river courses, the land on either side rising to high bluffs. Its streets are broad and shaded, and the architecture of its public and private buildings is tasteful, and in many cases elegant and costly."

The Daily Graphic (New York). 1878.

"I have never been in any town where so many people failed to draw their window shades, or owned green reading lamps, or sat by those green-shaded lamps and read. I looked into almost every house I passed,

and in all but two, I think, I saw the self-same picture of calm, literary domesticity."

Travel author JULIAN STREET. 1914.

"Yes, Kalamazoo is a spot on the map
And the passenger train stops there
And the factory smokestacks smoke
And the grocery stores are open
    Saturday nights
And the streets are free from
    citizens who vote
And inhabitants counted in the census.
Saturday night is the big night.
Listen with your ears on a Saturday
    night in Kalamazoo
And say to yourself: I hear America, I
    hear, what do I hear?"

CARL SANDBURG, from his poem "Sins of Kalamazoo." 1920.

"Its name has 'pleased the ear and tickled the fancy.'"

Kalamazoo Gazette. December 10, 1954.

Kalkaska (See p. 40)

Lake Linden

"This is the only town in my life I was in where the whole town had St. Vitus' Dance."

DR ALLEN RICE, describing the town in 1913. Lake Linden had huge stamping mills that crushed the copper-bearing rock. The heavy machines kept the town continuously shaking 24 hours a day, six days a week.

Lansing

See also *Architecture* (State Capital Building)

"Few people of today have ever questioned the moving of the capitol from

Kalkaska

"In what might be called the town square of Kalkaska, except that nearly all of the town is on one side and the railroad tracks are on the other, there is a statue. Not a confederate general, a Union general, an Indian chief, a bronzed howitzer or a limp tank. It is a trout. I am told that it is a brook trout and it is nearly twenty feet high. Curled and flexed, its enraged plaster strikes out of the smallish fountain at an imaginary giant fly, or more likely a worm dangling from worm heaven. Actually the fish looks like a cross between a smelt and a moray eel, or a sick alewife, with a tinge of green creeping along the dorsal and the dread spots beginning to appear."

JIM HARRISON. *Just Before Dark.* 1971.

TOM POWERS

Lansing (cont.)

Detroit to Lansing: but even fewer realize that there was actually no such thing as the village of Lansing when the measure was passed and signed."

From an 1847 issue of the *Lansing Journal*, quoted in *Lansing And Its Yesterdays.* 1930.

"When the Legislature of '47 was first organized the man who could have supposed it possible to wrest the capitol from Detroit and set it down in the midst of a dense forest on the banks of the Grand River would have been considered a fit subject for an insane asylum."

REP. ENOS GOODRICH, a member of the 1847 Legislature, in a speech to the Michigan Pioneer Society in 1880.

"What, shall we take the capitol from a large and beautiful city ... and stick it down in the woods and mud on the banks of the Grand River, amid choking miasma, ... where the howl of wolves and hissing of massaugas, and groans of bullfrogs resound to the hammer of the woodpecker."

MR. BISHOP, a legislator, arguing against moving the state capitol to Lansing. 1847.

"In case of invasion by a foreign foe, the Capitol of Michigan would be safe from attack. No enemy could ever prudently go as far into the interior for the purpose of destruction."

A Coldwater man arguing in favor of moving the Capitol from Detroit to Lansing. 1847.

"Almost as much trouble arose ... over naming the village that would grow up at the Capitol as was experienced in locating it. Among the names proposed were Harrison, Huron, Franklin, Washington, Fulton, LaFayette. Houghton, Kinderhook,

Marcellus, Rushridge, El Dorado, Thorbush, Wright, Tyler, Cass and Swedenborg."

M. M. QUAIFE, describing the situation in 1847. *Michigan: From Primitive Wilderness to Industrial Commonwealth.* 1948.

"Great Heavens! Only a few days ago Copper Harbor was suggested, but this is even a better joke — Lansing township, my oh, my!"

An unknown state legislator. 1847.

"The entire plat is about two miles long and one mile wide, embracing the whole of section sixteen and about half of nine and twenty-one. One year ago there was only one house, a barn and sawmill in the entire neighborhood and now there are more than a hundred scattered here and there among the trees forming on the whole a most grotesque appearance."

DAVID COCKRAN, in a letter from Lansing dated March 26, 1848.

"Yes! It is the broadest and deepest street I have ever seen."

MARK TWAIN's response to a Lansing civic booster who, on Twain's visit to Lansing in 1868, kept boasting of the magnificent broadness of Washington Ave.

"Back when I was growing up, the 'successful' Lansing Negroes were such as waiters and bootblacks. To be a janitor in some downtown store was to be highly respected. The real 'elite,' the 'big shots,' the 'voices of the race,' were the waiters at the Lansing Country Club and the shoeshine boys at the state capitol."

MALCOLM X, describing his view of the city as it was during the 1930s. *The Autobiography of Malcolm X.* 1965.

Leland

"The Leland area is a sort of Republican Key West packed full of Reaganite bliss-ninnies smirking over the recent tax cuts."

JIM HARRISON. *Just Before Dark.* 1980.

McBain

"Like Lake Wobegon, McBain is a little city that time forgot — and, indeed, time even forgot just when it originated."

RONALD JAGER. *Eighty Acres.* 1990

Mackinaw City

See also *Bridges* (Mackinac), *Islands* (Mackinac), *Military Forts* (Fort Michilimackinac) and *Natural Attractions* (Straits of Mackinac)

"... whenever the country is settled around the Straits it is likely to become a place of some importance."

JAMES STRANG. *Ancient and Modern Michilimackinac.* 1854.

"A little village chiefly important as a railroad terminus."

J. G. INGLIS. *Northern Michigan Handbook For Travelers.* 1898.

"Where else can you sit all day and still see the sun rise on one lake and set on another."

JEAN R. KOMAIKO, et al. *Around Lake Michigan.* 1980.

"People used to refer to us as just a parking lot for Mackinac Island."

BOB BARKER, Executive Director of the Mackinaw Area Tourist Bureau. 1989.

Mancelona

"In luck we trusted and now we are busted."

Mancelona Herald, reporting on the town's fire preparedness after a fire destroyed the town in 1868.

Manistee

"There is not even the charm of natural scenery to entice, nor the richness of soil to induce migration. ... The scenery presented was dreary and desolate."

Early description of the city from a long lost county history. 1800s.

"... Manistee is an old-fashioned lady with bustle and lots of trim."

DORIS SCHARFENBERG. *Long Blue Edge of Summer.* 1992.

Marquette

See also *Architecture* (Marquette Prison)

"Marquette, 1851-53, consisted of a few houses, a stumpy road winding along the lake shore; a forge which burned up after impoverishing its first owners; a trail westward, just passable for wagons, leading to another forge (still more unfortunate in that it did not burn), and to the developed iron hills beyond, with two or three hundred people uncertain of the future — they had fallen into the march of the century and were building better than they knew."

PETER WHITE, describing the city as it was during the early 1850s, in an address before the Pioneer Association of Michigan in 1885.

"Marquette exists today only in order to link the rest of the world to the iron mines located six to eight miles inland."

COLONEL CAMILLE PISANI. 1861.

"The excellent hotels afford ample accommodations for travelers and sojourners. The cool salubrious air brings health and vigor to the enervated frame. The speckled denizens of the mountain brooks tempt to piscatorial wanderings and gratify the epicurean appetite; while everywhere abound unbroken forest, the rugged hills, the rocky gorges, the impenetrable glens, the picturesque lakes and beautiful waterfalls, to delight the artist and, in the fullest measure afford to the lover of nature, in her wildest aspects, the enjoyment which he seeks."

Annual Report of the Commissioner of Mineral Statistics for the State of Michigan. 1877-78.

"As for Marquette, metropolis of the whole region, my most vivid recollection of the town in 1891 is Front Street's long row of saloons, broken only occasionally by a shoe store that displayed nothing but cruiser boots in its windows."

CARTER HARRISON. 1891.

"All the Upper Peninsula is like a spider's web reaching out to Marquette."

ALVIN DOTEN, describing the region in the 1840s. *God, Grit and Humor.* 1980.

"Queen City of the North."

KENNETH S. LOWE. *Motor News.* June 1962.

"... shopping center of the U.P."

DORIS SCHARFENBERG. *Country Roads of Michigan.* 1992.

Marshall

"One of the oldest, most 'homey' towns in the state."

WILLARD M. BRYANT, Secretary, Good Roads Association. *Michigan History Magazine*. July/October 1921.

"... the capital city of preservation in Michigan."

JOHN J. COLLINS. *Michigan History Magazine*. March/April 1986.

"Williamsburg of the Midwest."

Michigan Living. September 1986.

"Marshall makes the Midwest seem like the sweetest place on earth."

New York Times. June 23, 1991.

Marysville

"... a sleepy, decadent village, twenty years behind the time, without the inhabitants being aware of the fact. Its people were river pirates, and proud to be known as such. ..."

CLIFTON JOHNSON. *Highways and Byways of the Great Lakes*. 1911.

Mecosta

"... an odd little place left over from the logging days. ... The single street is so wide it makes the town seem abandoned much of the time; stores change hands, businesses come and go, and there seem to be no roots going out from it. When we were boys, we used to call it 'Brigadoon' and drive over now and then to see if it was still there."

CURTIS K. SLADTFIELD. *From the Land and Back*. 1972.

Meredith

"Meredith had a dismal end. It withered away and finally a big tobacco company offered a lot in the City of Meredith for a specified number of its famous brand of chewing tobacco."

STUART GROSS. *Indians, Jacks, and Pines*. 1962.

Midland

"... the town that Dow built. ..."

MEGAN SWOYER. *Michigan Living*. March 1989.

Milford

"... in 1832 ... no roads led to Milford."

SUE DAVIS LOWE. *Ten Minutes Ahead of the Rest of the World*. 1982.

"... the center of everything is Milford, Michigan. Because if you want to go to New York City, it's only 1,200 miles away. Chicago is 250 miles away, and it's 2,000 miles to Hollywood."

MARY JACKSON. 1981.

Monroe

"Legend has it that when Monroe's favorite son, General Custer, had left town on his way to the disaster at the Little Big

Horn, he had admonished the citizens not to do anything until he got back. Some of the more dour residents today claim that these instructions have been followed to the letter."

JOHN G. FULLER. *We Almost Lost Detroit.* 1975.

Mount Clemens

"One must conceive of the place as set down in an unbroken forest and made up of a half dozen or more log buildings, each with a small clearing above them and connected only by a rambling road which ran along the high points."

ROBERT F. ELDRIDGE, describing the area as it was in 1812. *Past and Present of Macomb County, Michigan.* 1905.

"... an all-year-round resort, full of life and gaiety."

CLYDE NEWNOM. *Michigan's Thirty-seven Million Acres of Diamonds.* 1927. Mt Clemens was famous around the turn of the century for its mineral waters and baths, which annually drew thousands of people.

Mount Pleasant

"Another Hub of Michigan has been found — Mount Pleasant. Circulars by the wholesale to this effect are being sent out. The city especially wants a toothpick factory and a clothespin mill. ..."

Detroit News. 1889.

Muskegon

"Lumber Queen of the World."

The name generally accorded to Muskegon in the 1880s. Numerous sources.

Negaunee

"It seems to me that Negaunee has more saloons to the acre than any other place in the United States."

From the diary of a trip to the U.P. in 1868 by R. A. BROTHERTON.

"Iron is the foster father and foster mother of Negaunee."

From the diary of a trip to the U.P. in 1868 by R. A. BROTHERTON.

"Some of the oldest settlers, old miners and their wives, declare that the town was laid out late on Christmas Eve by a drunken Scotch engineer during a howling blizzard, and that the only instrument he carried was a smoking lantern, while his lurching assistant carried a jug."

JOHN VOELKER. *Trouble-Shooter*, an autobiographical account of the author's life as a prosecutor in Marquette County. The fictionalized town Voelker calls Hematite in the book is Negaunee.

New Boston

"In New Boston three saloons operated seven days a week ... and on Sunday mornings the saloons outdrew the churches."

LARRY ENGELMANN, describing the city as it was during the 1870s. *Michigan History Magazine.* Summer 1977.

Niles

"Niles is a village of 1,100 or 1,200 inhabitants ... surrounded by a most beautiful country of openings and prairies. The settlement was commenced seven or eight years ago and it has been notorious even at the West for wickedness. The stores were open on the Sabbath and that was a great business day. The minister who formed the church ... told me once when he was preaching on the Sabbath at the sound of a flatboat horn coming down the river, all his male hearers but one left the house to see it."

Letter from REV. J. N. PARSONS of the American Home Missionary Society. 1840.

"Niles, on the St. Joseph, is a most difficult place to pass through, for the traveller always feels an irresistible impulse to remain there forever, — it is so charmingly situated, on such a charming stream, and inhabited by such charming people."

CHARLES LANMAN. *A Summer in the Wilderness.* 1847.

"When I entered a cellar and saw a rat reading the meter ahead of me, I accepted his reading and went on to the next house."

RING LARDNER, on reading meters for the Niles Gas Co. as a young man in 1905.

"I can't make up my mind which town I like best New York or Niles and it is hard to choose between the 2 of them on account of them being alike in so many ways. ... they both begin with N and both of thems got a Broadway and both of them so full of fords that your takeing your life in your hands when you cross acrost the street. And both of thems got a big river and lots of factorys and a fire dept."

RING LARDNER. *Chicago Tribune.* July 14, 1916.

Northport

"It seemed to us, as we gazed upon the beautiful scenery that met our eyes at every turn, that we had found the 'eldorado.' The forests were unbroken; the axe of the white man had not marred its beauty; the beach of the bay was not strewn with

refuse of the sawmill, but all lay in the state that Dame Nature had kept it, beautiful beyond description."

JAMES J. McLAUGHLIN, who settled near Northport in 1839.

Onaway

"The village of Onaway has no more need to be organized into a city than a dog needs two tails."

The *Presque Isle County Advocate*, editorializing on Onaway's attempt to become a city so it could become the Presque Isle County Seat in the early 1900s.

Ontonagon

"One cannot help fancying that he has gone to the ends of the earth, and beyond the boundaries appointed for the residence of man."

From the diary of HENRY SCHOOLCRAFT, written at the future site of the city on a trip to the U.P. in 1820.

"This wild Siberian end of the world, this queer country made by another hand from the rest of the common footstool, ... a cold, sterile region, bleak, barren and savage. ... there is not a spear of grass on a whole eternity of this country and an ox, turned out, would starve unless he could feed on pine shadows and moss."

Buffalo (New York) *Morning Express.* 1846.

Owosso

"I think it is the nicest place in the world. I was born there and I hope to die there. It's American, and it makes you feel at home."

JAMES OLIVER CURWOOD. 1920s.

"No negroes were allowed on the streets after dark. ... In point of fact, in those days lots of Michigan towns were like that."

MALCOLM X, describing the city in the 1940s. *The Autobiography of Malcolm X.* 1965.

"... most of Owosso, could serve as the location for a remake of any Andy Hardy movie."

THOMAS MALLON. *Rockets and Rodeos.* 1993.

Paradise

"... there is no sherbet in Paradise."

The response by a restaurant employee when photographers Ann and John Mahan stopped with their children in Paradise and asked for a dish of sherbet. 1986.

Peshabetown

"... the only pure indian village in Michigan."

PERRY POWERS. *A History of Northern Michigan and Its People.* 1912.

"The indians run a poker game near Peshabetown if you like poker with people who are looking to get even."

KURT LUEDTKE. *Michigan Living.* April 1987.

Petoskey

"The sunsets on the bay are enough to throw the artist's soul into ecstasy."

Unknown writer. circa 1865.

"This is a wonderfully bright little town, five or six years old, 'beautiful of situation,'

whence one may gaze out over the blue waters of the charming bay, and upon the distant and broader waters of Lake Michigan beyond, — and dream of peace without heat, dust, or discomfort of any sort but a crowded hotel."

A. JUDD NORTHRUP. *Camps and Tramps in the Adirondacks, and Grayling Fishing in Northern Michigan.* 1880.

"When dust is on the ragweed, and the ragweed's in yer nose,
    When yer nose is full o' sneezin', and the sneezin' full o' woes;
    Then's come the time to pack your duds and quickly git away;
    Petoskey is the Mecca then, why don't you come and stay?"

From the poem, "When Dust is on the Ragweed," by REV. WARREN W. LAMPOST. 1900s.

"... the most noted summer resort of Northern Michigan and one of the most popular in the country."

PERRY F. POWERS. *A History of Northern Michigan and Its People.* 1912.

"The city of million dollar sunsets."

Michigan Scenic Highways. 1933.

Plymouth

"... an epitome of most small communities of midwestern United States — a midwest microcosm."

SAM HUDSON. *The Story of Plymouth.* 1976.

Pontiac

"This whole region was then supposed to be an interminable morass, and so wild and dangerous was this expedition thought to be, that the party, before setting forth, took leave of their friends with all the solemnity befitting so grave an occasion."

BELA HUBBARD, Assistant State Geologist, describing the first party to explore the Pontiac area in 1817. An address before the Detroit Pioneer Society. January 1892.

"Twenty very neat and pretty houses, forming so many well furnished shops, a transparent stream, a clearing a quarter of a league square, and the eternal forest about: there is the faithful tableau of Pontiac which in twenty years, perhaps, will be a city."

ALEXIS DE TOCQUEVILLE. *Democracy in America.* 1831.

"The town is very pleasantly situated and seems to be a stirring place for business."

OLIVER HAZARD PERRY, describing the area in 1851. *Hunting Expeditions of Oliver Hazard Perry.* 1899.

"When folks ask where I was born, I sometimes reply I was born in Paradise, that is to say in Pontiac, Michigan. ..."

Historian ARTHUR POUND, who was born in Pontiac in 1884. *Michigan Alumunus Quarterly Review.* May 25, 1957.

"... a grimy city with anemic leadership, a dismal downtown where blocks of urban-renewal land sprouts weeds, and a combustible mixture of Southern whites, blacks, and Mexican-Americans."

NEAL PEIRCE. *The Megastates of America.* 1972.

Port Crescent

"With her large lumber manufactures, her salt industries, her fine location, and her excellent harbor facilities, with the rich country that surrounds her, we see no reason why Port Crescent should not grow and become one of the first towns in the country."

DR. EAKINS, the town doctor. 1869. Today, Port Crescent has disappeared and only an old mill chimney rises above the sands that cover the rest of the town.

Port Huron

"... a village of rude log huts."

CHANDLER GILMAN. *Life on the Lakes.* 1836.

Port Seldon

"Here once stood the proud city of Port Seldon, a victim of high jinx, high wines and high finance."

RALPH CHESTER MEIMA's 1921 epitaph for a Michigan ghost town that was founded 12 miles north of Holland in 1836 and had disappeared by the late 1840s.

Portland

"Portland is not so much a thing of the present, as an idea; a reality of the future. Neither a prophet, nor the son of a prophet, but the grandson of a deacon, the writer predicts that Portland will be the manufacturing town of the Grand River."

FRANKLIN EVERETT. *Memorials of the Grand River Valley.* 1878. Currently the town boasts a population of less than 4,000.

Remus

"Our town was an honest little place, with no pretensions and no right to any."

CURTIS K. SLADTFIELD, describing the city as it was in 1940. *From the Land and Back.* 1971.

Rochester

"We would like to see anything outside of Rochester that can beat us. With a population of about seven hundred, we are running a school with three departments, we have four churches, three literary societies, two splendid flouring mills, one of the largest paper mills in the country, a woolen factory, a plaster mill, a foundry, a jeweler, a photographer, a printing office, some of the best piano players, singers, the smartest business men, the most fashionable ladies, the best housekeepers, the handsomest girls, the fastest horses, the rarest breed of dogs and more candidates for office than any other town can boast."

T. B. FOX, a Rochester resident. 1874.

Rogers City

"... a forest primeval of white and Norway pines, only here and there a clearing large enough for a tent or a log house or a hut of rough board."

An 1870 description of Rogers City by an unknown traveler.

Saginaw

See also *Bridges* (Zilwaukee)

"... only Indians, muskrats, and bull frogs could live in Saginaw."

MAJOR DANIEL BAKER, reporting on the living conditions at a fort on the present site of Saginaw. 1822.

"You want to go to Saginaw! ... do you realize what you are undertaking? Do you know that Saginaw is the last inhabited place til the Pacific Ocean; that from here to Saginaw hardly anything but wilderness and pathless solitudes are to be found?"

A Pontiac innkeeper to Alexis de Tocqueville, on hearing that the French traveler was journeying to Saginaw. 1831.

"We were taken to one of three houses that make up Saginaw ... an area of cultivation in the midst of savage tribes and impenetrable forest.

... thirty persons, men, women, old people, and children at the time of our visit composed this little society, as yet scarcely formed — an opening seed thrown upon the desert, there to germinate."

ALEXIS DE TOCQUEVILLE. 1831.

"The east bank of the Saginaw River was the most unlikely spot for a city that Michigan could offer."

STUART GROSS, describing his view of the area as it was in the 1840s. *Indians, Jacks, and Pines.* 1962.

"A rude hamlet of shanties, planted on the edge of a swamp."

JEHUDI ASHMUN, an early Saginaw settler. 1852.

"From a struggling, almost forgotten settlement on the edge of an unbroken forest in 1850, Saginaw County had grown to almost 70,000 persons (by 1879). There were more saloons and prostitutes than doctors and dentists, and the lumber barons and rich merchants were content to leave it that way."

STUART GROSS. *Frankie and the Barons.* 1991.

"... one of the ugliest spots in America."

RICHARD REEVES, describing the view from the Bancroft Hotel in Saginaw. *American Journey.* 1982.

St. Ignace

"In these days when patriotic chambers of commerce label every whistle-stop the gateway to something or other, St. Ignace is with daring originality hailed the 'Gateway to the North.'"

JOHN VOELKER. *Trouble-shooter.* 1943.

"... visit(ors) ... were usually so harassed after a long wait for the Mackinac ferry that the sign, 'You are now leaving St. Ignace,' was the only sight the travelers were eager to see."

A description of the city during the 1950s by BRADY BENSON. *Motor News.* July 1989.

"... St. Ignace, front door to Michigan's Upper Peninsula."

ANDREW H. BROWN. *National Geographic.* March 1952.

"Welcome to St Ignace — Founded 1671 — Reborn 1957."

City limits signs posted on the borders of the town that reflected the city's rebirth with the opening of the Mackinac Bridge in 1957.

"... among the least-known cities of historic importance in the nation."

BRADY BENSON. *Motor News.* July 1959.

"St. Ignace is the tourist capital of the U.P. It is a summer place for people who like to spend Saturday nights looking at doodads and souvenir birchbark canoes."

JOHN G. MITCHELL. *Audubon Magazine.* November 1981.

St. Joseph

"At 4 o'clock we reached the marsh which surrounds St. Joseph. Figure to yourself a pestilential black mud, quivering and shaking under its own weight, with tufts of grass, rank and uneven, a deep river in the midst and sand banks where the mud ceases. Rising from this was a steep but small bluff extending into the lake, on which the city stands. Two handsome houses built in 1837 and, I believe now empty, two large wooden taverns, one now untenanted, and a few other indifferent looking places with some stray houses along the river, complete the coup de' ceil of this famous city which had sprung up in a night and withered next day."

From a letter by JOHN FORBES, president of the Michigan Central Railroad. 1847.

Saugatuck

GARY W. BARFKNECHT

"Provincetown, Mass., without Portuguese."

JEAN R. KOMAIKO, et al. *Around Lake Michigan.* 1980.

Sault Ste. Marie

See also *Rivers* (St. Mary's River) and *Soo Canal*

"The fag end of the world."

BARON L' HONTAN of the French Army describing the Sault after he visited in 1688.

"The situation of the village is pleasing and romantic; the ground rises gently from the edge of the river, the houses, if they merit that name, are scattered irregularly over the ridge, to within four hundred yards of the fall."

JOHN JOHNSON. *An Account of Lake Superior*. 1807.

"It was a place of extremes in almost everything, including the climate."

MRS. ANGELINE BINGHAM GILBERT, recalling her childhood in the Sault in the 1830s.

"... too rough a place to bring up a family."

ABRAHAM WARREN WILLIAMS, the first white settler at Grand Island on why he left the Sault. 1830s.

"(The) remotest settlement in the United States, if not in the moon."

U.S. SENATOR HENRY CLAY. 1839.

"Two or three years ago this settlement of the Sault Ste Marie was but a military post of the United States, in the midst of a village of Indians and half-breeds. ... Five years hence, the primitive character of the place will be altogether lost. ..."

WILLIAM CULLEN BRYANT, in a letter dated August 15, 1846.

"I had placed my standard too low with regard to the Sault Ste. Marie, that I was not less surprised than delighted to behold it occupying a situation so commanding and beautiful."

ROBERT E. CLARKE. *Harpers Magazine*. March 1853.

"This old and much neglected town can boast of beautiful Rapids, the St. Mary's River here having a descent of twenty feet within one mile, a Ship Canal, with two locks ... some dilapidated wharves, and the grounds on which stand Fort Brady ... one well-kept hotel of modest pretensions, where thousands have been entertained during the past twelve years since the completion of the canal. Yet it has not progressed for that period either in population or in any kind of improvements: the streets, stores and dwelling-houses in many cases being neglected and suffered to go to decay."

J. DISTURNELL. *The Great Lakes or Inland Seas of America*. 1868.

"With the exception of the missionary history of St. Ignace, the military history of Mackinac and the ancient mining history of the Ontonagon, Houghton, Keweenaw and Isle Royale Copper Districts, there is not a locality in the whole Northwest which yields more interesting historical subject than this village."

History of the Upper Peninsula of Michigan. 1883.

"Thousands of eyes have been attracted by the prominent and important location of Sault Ste. Marie, Mich., the hub of the central North, the city with a great future, surrounded, as it is by many of the greatest natural advantages ever bestowed upon on earthly region."

C. S. OSBORN. *The Soo*. 1887.

"Sault Ste. Marie is a town as old as Boston, but it still is primitive. Its streets end in a darkness of spruce and hemlock or in an emptiness of water. In winter, it is locked in white silence."

WALTER HAVINGHURST. *Land of Promise*. 1946.

"Away from the tourist attractions the town lives its private life on the back roads and the side streets, much the same as fifty years ago."

STEPHEN A. BLOSSOM. *Inland Seas*. Spring 1983.

Seney

• In the 1890s Seney became famous as the roughest lumber town in northwoods. During its 15-year heyday it was known as Helltown U.S.A.

"Strangers were met at the train, upended, and shaken until their pockets were emptied. Saloon entertainers counted biting the heads off live frogs and snakes among their minor talents. Eye-gouging, biting off ears, gambling, gun battles — it was a nail-hard town."

A description of the area in the 1890s by ALIDA MALKUS. *Blue-Water Boundary.* 1960.

"Into its brief fifteen years of existence it compressed a hundred years' sin and hell-raising."

JOHN MARTIN, describing the town as it was in the 1890s. *Call it North Country.* 1944.

"Seney did rear something besides bums, lumberjacks, swindlers, murders and the like. ... It was just an ordinary community like any other in America — just a little rougher around the edges!"

A description of the town during the 1890s by JOHN T. RIORDAN. *The Dark Peninsula.* 1976.

"On my first Christmas ... I worked all day and all night treating the fighters who could find their way to my office by following the red trail on the snow that reddened and broadened as the day wore on. I doubt there was anywhere another town like Seney as it was in the nineties. I have seen the streets and the board sidewalks of the town literally swamped with fighting loggers."

DR. FRANK P. BOHN, the town's first doctor. 1890s.

"... an inconspicuous cluster of houses and stores at the junction of State Highways 28 and 77."

JIM DOHERTY. *Audubon Magazine.* September 1984

Tawas City

"... it is impossible to step out on the street without hearing a volley of blasphemy, or seeing some whiskey soaked wretch reeling along, ... saloon fights are almost a daily occurance, and encounters with deadly weapons are occasional happenings; ... vice stalks unrebuked on our most public thoroughfare, and openly defies the law."

The *Iosco County Gazette,* editorializing on the decline of morals in the city. 1870.

Tecumseh

"... thirty miles beyond Monroe and forty miles beyond God's blessing."

A native of Tecumseh describing the location of his town. 1830s.

"I write from the most charming inland town in Michigan. For picturesque beauty and quiet, pretty scenery, it is in my opinion without a rival."

From a letter written to a Minneapolis newspaper by M. W. H. W. in the 1850s.

Thompson

"Blink an eye and you have entered and left town."

JEAN R. KOMAIKO, et al. *Around Lake Michigan.* 1980.

Thompsonville

"... the most pleasant and most favored spot for a prosperous town in all the broad expanse of Michigan's great peninsula."

Hyperbole from the Thompsonville Improvement Association. 1893.

"The biggest Little Town in Michigan."

Self promotion from the Thompsonville Chamber of Commerce. 1901.

Traverse City

"The objective point of our journey was ultimately reached, although the most vivid imagination could not have associated the place with the name it had assumed. The city part was wholly prospective, and to our limited view too far distant ever to be realized."

REV. S. STEELE, commenting on his arrival in Traverse City in 1859.

"To the right rose a bank of woods; to the left, a range of forest; to the rear the island stood defined. And in front of us there was a notch in the monotony of the timbered landscape — as if a snag-toothed giant had humorously bitten a piece out of the shoreline and disliked the flavor of it.

'There it is,' said my father, watching me closely. 'That is Traverse City.'

'I don't see any city,' said I."

THOMAS BATES, the future editor of the *Grand Traverse Herald*, recalling his first impression of Traverse City. 1862.

"And so we saw Traverse City, Michigan. The less said about it the better."

From Governor William Milliken's grandfather's diary. The 1873 entry records his first day in the city.

"I have been asked to tell something of society in Traverse City in the early days. It would be difficult to tell of a thing which did not exist, and there was certainly nothing which could have answered to that name."

ADA K. SPRAGUE PRATT. 1870s.

"All accounts agree in the statement that, before the so-called improvements of civilization had marred the adornments of nature, this was a most beautiful spot."

DR. M. L. LEACH. *A History of the Grand Traverse Region.* 1883.

"It's wonderful, suckers at the front door and suckers at the back."

Famed silent screen actor WILLIAM S. HART's observation while standing at the back door of Steinberg's Grand Opera House, which backed up to the Boardman River. 1900s.

"At the turn of the century it was a lumbering community of approximately six thousand people. There were 14 churches and 21 saloons. Three recognized bordellos and a lot of rough young people ready to keep things on the hum. Sin was in the saddle for sexes."

AL BARNES, describing the area as it was in 1900. *Let's Fly Backwards.* 1976.

"... I do believe that we will see the time when Traverse City will reach ... twenty thousand inhabitants."

Traverse City lumber baron PERRY HANNAH. 1900s.

"The quality of life in Traverse City would be hard to give up. I'm where everyone else wants to be. I rarely take a vacation in the summer; where else would I go that could be better than this."

KEITH CHARTERS, part owner of Embers on the Bay in Traverse City. 1989.

GARY W. BARFKNECHT

"... Michigan's miniature-golf capital."

GARY BARFKNECHT. *Ultimate Michigan Adventures.* 1989. As of 1989 there were a total of 72 holes of miniature golf on a 1¼ mile stretch of US-31 just east of Traverse City.

"A place where you don't have to give up a good living to live a good life."

Outside Magazine. July 1992. The magazine ranked Traverse City ninth among the top 10 best places to live in the U.S.

Trenary

"What Detroit is to cars and Hershey, Pa. is to acne, Trenary is to cinnamon toast."

NEAL RUBIN. *Detroit Free Magazine.* May 10, 1992. The Trenary House Bakery in the tiny U.P. town packages cinnamon toast that is sent as far away as California and Alaska.

Warren

"From a tourist standpoint, Warren certainly is no attraction and doesn't care to be. ..."

RUSS FULLER. *Motor News.* October 1967.

Westland

"Westland is a workingman's community, functional if it's nothing else, and nothing else is exactly what it is."

LOREN ESTLEMAN. *Lady Yesterday.* 1987.

White Pigeon

"White Pigeon ... stands on an extensive prairie which, for miles about, presents such attractions as to have riveted many English farmers to the spot."

CATHERINE STEWART. *New Homes in the West.* 1843.

Climate

"Don't go to Michigan, that land of ills;
That word means ague, fever and chills."

A common 1820s rhyme.

"I think with the favor of Providence that I shall now be able to get through in spite of the intolerable heat of the atmosphere — and you may be sure it is hot as you can possibly conceive of — The furnace in which they undertook to bake Shadrack and his fellows in the old times is no comparison at all — this Michigan sun would scorch them to a cinder in twenty minutes."

AUSTIN BLAIR, in a letter from Jackson in the summer of 1841, shortly after he arrived from New York state.

"In this uncertain climate the hopes of the eager watcher for spring are doomed to many and many a disappointment."

BELA HUBBARD.*Memorials of a Half-Century in Michigan and the Lakes Region.* 1888.

"Michigan is the favored state of the North Temperate Zone, for its climate is thoroughly air-conditioned and thermostatically controlled by the waters of the Great Lakes."

Federal Writers Project. *Michigan: A Guide to the Wolverine State.* 1941.

"Michiganians, unlike residents of Florida or California, are not likely to boast of the climate."

WILLIS F. DUNBAR, GEORGE S. MAY. *Michigan: A History of the Wolverine State.* 1970.

"There is an old saying on the lakes. 'If you don't like the weather, wait five minutes, it will change.' "

WILLIAM RATIGAN. *Great Lakes Shipwrecks and Survivals.* 1977. This old saying has been repeated so often by so many people that it has become a cliche.

"... there's still a fine line between Michigan and misery — winter."

SONNY ELIOT. *Michigan Living.* September 1988.

Counties

Allegan County

"When Mother Nature was handing out the scenery, Allegan County took a little of everything. ..."

Advertising copy promoting the county. Source and date unknown.

Barry County

"The only upper peninsula county in the lower peninsula."

A common saying among county residents because of its sparse population, hundreds of lakes, and thousands of acres of swamp and woodland. 1980s.

Bay County

"... the scenery became so wild and forbidding, the county so poor, that a century must certainly elapse before the crowded people of the east, in desperation, would seek homes in this remote section."

An unknown land surveyor, recording his impressions of the area around Saginaw Bay. 1830s.

"From Bay City we passed through a flat, wooded, and exceedingly uninteresting country."

A. JUDD NORTHRUP. *Camps and Tramps in the Adirondacks and Grayling Fishing in Northern Michigan.* 1880.

Berrien County

"'Tis a spot, the best adapted of any to be seen, for the purpose of living."

Unknown French officer. 1718.

"A region that almost merits the lofty appellation of the Garden of America."

JAMES FENIMORE COOPER. 1840s.

Chippewa County

"Suffice it to say that Chippewa County ... contains a vast acreage of as rich farming land as the sun ever kissed."

C.S. OSBORN. *The Soo.* 1887.

Clare County

"The Bull's-eye of lower Michigan."

North Eastern Michigan. April 1916.

Gogebic County

"Nothing can exceed the desolate solitude of this region. ... Its stillness is never broken, except by the crashing of the tornado through the dense forest tearing up the trees, and piling them together, so as if still further to repel the intrusion of man into a region, so little fitted for his reception."

A description by two early visitors to the county in 1850.

Hillsdale County

"Hillsdale county ... abounds in the most beautiful natural park scenery you can conceive. A more lovely undulating country, covered with rich grass, interspersed with forest or groups of trees, and varied by limpid lakes, we never beheld."

CHARLES LATROBE. *The Rambler in North America.* 1832.

Ingham County

"This county, for a new county was considerably advanced. ... One could even get to a railroad in four or five days. ..."

JOHN W. LONGYEAR, an early settler in the county. 1840.

Iron County

"Did you hear about the farmer up the road? He's dead, you know. He tripped and fell off one of his fields and was killed."

A popular joke in Iron County around the turn of the century that made fun of the hardships of trying to farm the county's rough and rocky terrain.

Kalkaska County

"Driving around Kalkaska County, you are reminded of those Jonathon Winters' routines involving a hound with a bald tail

sleeping near a gas pump and chickens scratching in a bare yard."

JIM HARRISON. *Just Before Dark.* 1971.

Leelanau County

"In this locale, winter begins in October and runs unremittingly until the end of March. My friend in warmer climes won't believe we had sixteen and a half feet of snow this year. After a while you no longer believe there's any earth left under the snow. The ground is a fib."

JIM HARRISON. *Just Before Dark.* 1972.

"It's out of your way. No matter where you are going, Leelanau County is not on the way to it unless you are in Leelanau County already, in which case you must either go back the way you came or get seriously wet."

KURT LUEDTKE. *Michigan Living.* April 1987.

"Leelanau County is that end of the rainbow kind of place."

BEVERLY GILMORE of Glen Arbor. 1989.

"We are, of course, somewhat isolated on the Leelanau Peninsula — geographically, and in other ways as well, which is not the same thing as living without cognizance of what's going on. Living on the Leelanau Peninsula is a little like staying back home when there's a war on: we hear what's happening at the Front, but we aren't there."

KATHLEEN STOCKING. *Letters From the Leelanau.* 1989.

"When Manhattenites start moving into the midwestern backwaters, into a nowhere northern Michigan peninsula like the Leelanau, you know something's happening to the country's demographics. It's too soon to say what, but the feeling you have watching it is similar to seeing geese flying north in November: it's not what you expect."

KATHLEEN STOCKING. *Letters From the Leelanau.* 1989.

"Sadly, Leelanau is one of those wonderland areas endangered by its own appeal."

DORIS SCHARFENBERG. *County Roads of Michigan.* 1992.

Marquette County

"The U. P. in general and (Marquette County) in particular constitutes one of the best hunting and fishing regions in Michigan and perhaps rivals any in fishing."

ROBERT TRAVER. *Small Town D. A.* 1954.

Mason County

"In the days when pine was king of Northern Michigan, Mason County was one of the monarch's most powerful provinces."

PERRY F. POWERS. *A History of Northern Michigan and Its People.* 1912.

Muskegon County

"Welcome to Muskegon County, where the taxes are going higher and higher."

A billboard on US-31. 1960s.

Ontonagon County

"Every object tells us that it is a region alike unfavorable to the productions of the animal or vegetable kingdoms, and we shudder in casting our eyes over the frightful wreck of trees, and the confused groups of falling-in banks and shattered stones, yet we have only to ascend these bluffs to behold hills more rugged and elevated, and the dark hemlock forests, and yawning gulfs more dreary and more forbidding to the eye."

HENRY SCHOOLCRAFT. 1830s.

Presque Isle County

"It was conceded by the whole survey party, that the entire tract that we had surveyed was worthless; the government would never realize enough from the sale of the lands to pay for the surveying."

D. D. OLIVER, a member of the party that surveyed the county in 1839.

"... the amount of fish and game in Presque Isle County preclude the possibility of anyone's starving as long as they can hold a fish pole or handle a gun."

Presque Isle County Advance. 1878.

Saginaw County

"Taking into consideration the abundance of wild game, fish and waterfowl, the great fertility of the soil, the kindly deposition of the Indians, and the social enjoyments among the white settlers, I think there was no place in Michigan where pioneer life could be more easily sustained or better enjoyed than at Saginaw."

A description of the area in 1833 by JUDGE ALBERT MILLER. *Michigan Pioneer Collection,* VIII. 1886.

"In my journey from to Detroit to Saginaw in January of the year I was not pleased with the appearance of the County of Saginaw. It was wet, open winter, and the passage from Flint to Saginaw was made in a huge uncomfortable wagon, sometimes through water and deep muck, and a considerable amount of the way over corduroy roads. The whole country about Saginaw seemed to me to be one vast swamp and did not impress me favorably."

NORMAN LITTLE, recalling his arrival in Saginaw in 1850.

St. Joseph County

"Tis a spot, the best adapted of any to been seen, for purposes of living. There are pheasants as in France; quails and paroquets, the finest vines in the world which produce a vast quantity of very excellent grapes. It is the richest district in all the country."

FATHER LOUIS HENNEPIN. 1718.

"Ask he who thrives the country back?
Let him just ride to Pontiac;
Or take the stage to Washtenaw,
The finest land he ever saw,
Except St. Joseph's, where 'tis said,
Is where Paradise was laid.
St. Joseph's now is a disease,
Which emigration seems to seize,
And carries off, at sundry times,
Whole families — to distant climes,
Where fertile counties proudly claim
Old Hickory's and Van Buren's name."

Poet unknown. 1830.

Fauna

Black Bears

"The late Archie Dunlap, of Newberry, Michigan, who spent fifty years of his long life handling animals in circuses told me that he considered Michigan black bears (the semi-domesticated variety) the 'most potentially dangerous animals' he'd ever seen."

JOHN T. NEVILL. *Wanderings: Sketches of Northern Michigan Yesterday and Today.* 1955.

Black Flies

"Porcupine Mountain bears."

Upper Peninsula slang for black flies. 1957.

Brook Trout

"Trying to describe a fresh-caught brook trout is about as easy as trying to describe a sunset."

JOHN VOELKER. *Michigan Living.* April 1990.

General

"The country is well stocked with stags, wild goat, and bears, all of which furnish excellent food, and they are not at all fierce as in other countries. There are herds of buffalos that trample down the flowers and grass as they rush around in clumsy motion. There are great numbers of moose and elk, which in size of their horns almost rival the branches of the great trees. Turkey cocks sweep along like clouds overhead."

FATHER LOUIS HENNEPIN, observing the wildlife along the Detroit River in 1679.

"Bears, beavers, otters, wolverines, porcupines, panthers besides numerous smaller animals abound in the State. In the northern parts of the peninsula numerous herds of elk traverse the silent landscape; and in winter it is not unfrequent to see packs of wolves in pursuit of the deer across the crusts of snow."

JAMES W. LANMAN. *History of Michigan.* 1839.

Grayling

• This magnificent game fish was principally found in the Au Sable and Muskegon rivers. It had become extinct in Michigan by the 1930s due to overfishing and the destruction of its habitat by logging operations.

"In 1871, a party along the Au Sable caught so many grayling that they left more than two thousand on the shore to rot."

BRUCE RUBENSTEIN and LAWRENCE ZIEWACZ. *Michigan: A History of the Great Lakes State.* 1981.

"The sport he affords his capture, the taste he gratifies in the frying pan, and the allurements of the charming streams he inhabits, all conspire with his simplicity to destroy him."

A. JUDD NORTHRUP. *Camps and Tramps in the Adirondacks, and Grayling Fishing in Northern Michigan.* 1880.

"That article just now going the rounds of the press about the grayling disappearing in the Au Sable is a genuine concentrated lie."

Grayling Avalanche. 1881.

"The average length of this beauty is about ten inches; but he has the strength and dash and gameness of a young whale."

Michigan Central Railroad. *The Fairy Isle of Mackinac.* 1888.

"The grayling were such ravenous feeders, if you didn't catch fifty to one hundred and fifty you didn't think it was a very good day's fishing."

ESBERN HANSON, an early and well-known fisherman on the Au Sable. 1900s.

"There is no species sought by anglers that surpasses the grayling for beauty."

DAVID STARR JORDAN. *North American Food and Game Fishes.* 1902.

"Doubtless God could make a better fish than the Michigan grayling but doubtless He never did."

WILLIAM B. MERSHON, an early twentieth century conservationist. 1920s.

"My experience has taught me that ounce for ounce in weight, the grayling will try your tackle one-half more than the brook trout or any other Michigan fish,

with the possible exception of the black bass."

WILLIAM B. MERSHON. *Recollections of Fifty Years of Hunting and Fishing.* 1923.

"We used to fish with three, and sometimes with four flies attached to the leader, and catches of three and four at a cast were not infrequent. I once caught twelve grayling at five successive casts; mind I say casts, making two triple catches and three double catches."

WILLIAM B. MERSHON. *Recollections of Fifty Years of Hunting and Fishing.* 1923.

"The grayling lay like cordwood in the Au Sable, and it was no trick to catch them on a fly tied with the feathers of a blue jay or a highholer or a squirrel."

RUBE BABBITT. *Detroit News.* December 15, 1929.

"Mother Nature was kind to Michigan in many ways, but in no way greater than in providing for the unique and beautiful game fish called the grayling."

EUGENE T. PETERSON, outdoor writer and conservationist. 1974.

Kirtland's Warbler

• One of the world's rarest birds, it wasn't discovered until 1851 and its nesting area in the northcentral Lower Peninsula remained a mystery until 1903. Presently there are just over 200 breeding pairs in the world.

"Ounce for ounce, the Kirtland's Warbler has drawn more official interest and created more controversy than any other songbird in history."

A Bird of Fire, Kirtland's Warbler. Date unknown.

Lampreys

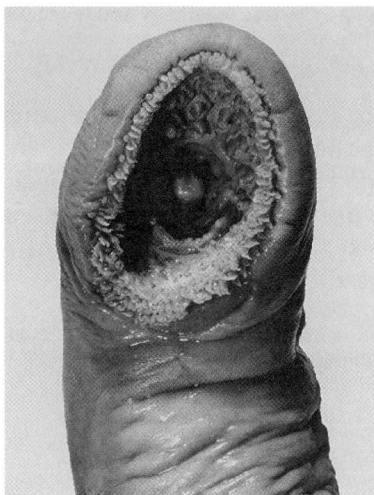

FLINT PUBLIC LIBRARY

"Investigations will be made to determine possible utilization of sea lampreys as food. New Englanders prized them as such in colonial days, and Henry I, of England died as a result of over-indulgence in them at a banquet."

Detroit News. November 3, 1946.

FLINT PUBLIC LIBRARY

Kirtland's Warbler

Mice

"I am so overrun with deer mice that I can hardly live in the woods. They eat the Strings of my tent, my Shoes, Pork, Hard bread, Gloves, leather strings, Bags, etc., and commenced last night working in my hair, and planting their cold noses on the scalp of my head."

OLIVER HAZARD PERRY. *Hunting Expeditions of Oliver Hazard Perry.* 1899. The incident happened in 1853 on a hunting trip in the Thumb area.

Mosquitoes

"... sucking the life's blood out of us every night. These infernals would get into cracks and crevices of the log castles, and nothing but hell-fire and brimstone would remove them."

A settler in the early 1800s complaining about the mosquitoes, fleas and bedbugs.

"Inexpressible torment caused by the mosquitoes."

From notes made by ALEXIS DE TOCQUEVILLE near Saginaw. 1831.

"The musquitoes and gnats ... are more numerous and more voracious than I have ever met with elsewhere. I do not doubt that their number is sufficient, upon every quarter of an acre, to consume the last drop of blood in my entire company."

Land surveyor LEWIS CLASON, in a letter he wrote while working north of Saginaw Bay and which he addressed from "Musquito Headquarters." 1837.

"(Mosquitoes here are) thick enough to stir with a stick."

CHARLES HINKLE of Allegan County in 1837.

"(Michigan mosquitoes) are enough to make Philosophy go hang herself, and Patience swear like a Turk. ..."

ANNA BROWNELL JAMESON. *Winter Studies and Summer Rambles.* 1839.

"I had heard much and much was I fore-warned, but never could have conceived the torture they can inflict, nor the impossibility of escape, defence, or endurance. Some amiable person who took an especial interest in our future welfare, in enumerating the torments prepared for hardened sinners, assures us that they will be stung by mosquitoes all made of brass, and as large as black beetles — he was an ignoramus and bungler; you may credit me, that the brass is quite an unnecessary improvement, and the increase of size equally superfluous. Mosquitoes as they exist in this upper world are as pretty and perfect a plague as the most ingenious amateur sinner-tormentor ever devised."

ANNA BROWNELL JAMESON. *Winter Studies and Summer Rambles.* 1839.

"These insects are the curse of the American wilderness. ... I never felt the torments such those which I suffered from them during the whole of this expedition, and especially at Saginaw. In the day they prevented us from drawing, or writing, or sitting still for an instant; in the night thousands of them buzzed around us settling on every spot on our bodies that was uncovered."

ALEXIS DE TOCQUEVILLE. *Memoirs and Remains of de Tocqueville,* Vol. 1. 1843.

"Mosquitoes were one of the torments of early settlers for they had no screen doors or screens for windows. As dusk came on they would make a smudge by putting damp chips in a pan and setting fire to them. This pan placed in front of a door would make a smoke screen which kept pests out. Soon after I was married we had a screen door which was the first seen in this neighborhood."

A Michigan farm wife recalling rural life in 1866.

"And, lastly though by no means least, during the summer season, which is the only one in which work can be done at all, forests are so full of venomous insects that it is next to impossible for any instrument to be used."

From the annual report of GENERAL REYNOLDS, who was in charge of surveying Michigan in 1866.

"Keweenaw Eagles."

U.P. slang for mosquitoes. WILLIAM RATIGAN. *Straits of Mackinac.* 1957.

"Growing up in northern Michigan, I got to know insects intimately. I prided myself on my ability to tolerate gnats and black-flies. ... But I had never seen mosquitoes like those that rose that day from the weeds and grasses along the Fox River. ... Even when I sprayed the aerosol directly at them they scarcely altered their flight. They absorbed the poison and developed genetic immunity right before my eyes."

JERRY DENNIS. *A Place on the Water.* 1993.

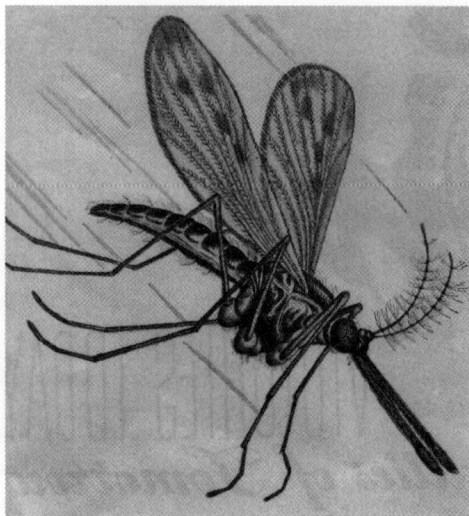

Passenger Pigeons

• The last passenger pigeon in Michigan was seen in 1898, and the last passenger pigeon in the world died in a Ohio zoo in 1914.

"... we came to the pigeon roost. Pigeon dung covered the ground, looking like a heavy fall of grayish snow; flowers, shrubs, underwood, and small trees were dead as if fire had swept through the woods, and thousands of large trees might as well have been girdled by the axe; great limbs were scattered about as though a tornado had followed the fire. The ground was strewn with bodies of pigeons, killed by accident in the gathering of the great assemblage. Mingled with the dead pigeons were countless numbers of pure white eggs. The smell of dead birds and rotten eggs added to that of the dung, so that all that breathed were threatened with suffocation. The noise was so great that we could speak to one another only by shouting, cooings of pigeons were to my ears moans of pain; whirring wings sounded like the coming of a storm. These continuous noises were punctuated by the fall of limbs overweighted with pigeons."

U. P. HENDRICK. *The Land of the Crooked Tree.* 1948. An eyewitness account of one of the last great nestings of passenger pigeons in Michigan near Petoskey in 1870.

"... at Petoskey in 1878 ... at least one-million birds were killed or captured."

EUGENE T. PETERSON in *Michigan Perspectives: People, Events, and Issues by Alan Brown.* 1974.

"Imagine if you can a tract of land about sixteen miles long and three miles wide, where every bough is occupied by a dozen nests and a hundred birds; where the air whirs from dawn til dark with ceaseless wings; where the flights that settle cover square acres with a living carpet; where from 250 to 400 men have for six weeks or more been engaged in trapping and killing without cessation, and yet not made the numbers appreciably less; imagine 50 square miles of pigeons, and that is the scene."

A *New York World* correspondent describing a passenger pigeon roost near Frankfort in June of 1874.

"It was proverbial with our fathers, that if the Great Spirit in his wisdom could have created a more elegant bird in plummage, form, and movement, He never did. I have stood for hours admiring the movements of these birds, I have seen them fly in unbroken lines from the horizon, one line succeeding another from morning until night ... I have stood by the greatest waterfall in America and regarded the descending torrents in wonder and astonishment, yet never have my astonishment, wonder, and admiration been so stirred as when I have witnessed these birds drop from their course like meteors from heaven."

SIMON POKAGON, Chief of the Southern Michigan Potawatomi. 1880s.

"There have been few birds in the history of Michigan, indeed in the history of mankind, that have captured the imagination as did the passenger pigeon. Old timers who have seen a flight of pigeons were hard pressed to find words to describe the scene. Such enormous numbers of birds passing overhead would blot out the noonday sun, and for hours it would be as dark as midnight."

EUGENE T. PETERSON in *Michigan Perspectives: People, Events, and Issues* by Alan Brown. 1974.

Seagull

"Those gulls that strolled the beach at Tawas Bay would eat anything. Anything. Anytime. Apples, hot dogs, smoked herring, Michigan dill pickles, Jewish dill pickles, garlic dill pickles. Name it, they'd eat it.

They'd eat it even if it didn't have a name."

HAZEL GIRARD. *Blow for Battens Crossing.* 1979.

Sturgeon

"Saginaw beef."

Saginaw area slang for sturgeon in the 1880s.

"A six footer weighing a hundred pounds was considered a good catch, but the Michigan record-holder tipped the beam at 327 pounds and he lost his last fight, not with a spear, but with the propeller of a lake freighter with which he had disputed the right of way."

WILLIAM RATIGAN. *Straits of Mackinac.* 1957.

"Sturgeon were so thick in the lakes (in 1881) as to be a genuine nuisance. Their carcasses were taken from the nets set for more desirable species, piled on the beaches in great maharajan pyres and torched. Steamboat firemen fueled the boilers with them. Now they are next to extinct."

WILLIAM ASHWORTH. *The Late Great Lakes.* 1987.

Turkey

"I wish the bald eagle had not been chosen as the representative of our country; he is a bird of bad moral character; like those among men who live by sharping and robbing, he is generally poor, and often very lousy. The turkey is a much better respectable bird, and withal a true original native of America."

BEN FRANKLIN. 1770s.

"There are so many turkey's that twenty or thirty could be killed in one shot."

CADILLAC, founder of Detroit. 1700s.

"Boy, Turkey hunting. It's really something. Know what I mean?
I mean, you do everything just the way its supposed to be done and nothing happens. Then some guy tells you about getting out of his car, walking 25 yards into the woods, seeing a turkey, shooting him and then he wants to know what the big deal is."

BOB GWIZDZ. *Flint Journal.* May 14, 1966.

White-tailed deer

"We could not meet a man in the country all about that had ever seen a small deer. The word fawn, from desuetude, will be dropped from the language. It was always 'the blankest biggest buck! blank me!' or 'the blank, blankest, blank of a blank doe! running like a blank and blankation for the blank river!' That was all we could get; and when perchance one of these identical, peculiarly qualified animals happened to be shot, the speaker stood wholly unabashed and unconscious in the presence of his refutation. It must be in the climate."

Scribners.. April 1878.

"The deer in our county have absolutely no respect for law enforcement and frankly we're sick of it."

SERGEANT MIKE DISCHER of the Calhoun County Sheriff's Office, on his county's 1,368 deer-car accidents, the second-highest county total in the state for 1991.

Whitefish

"This sort of white fish, in my opinion, is the only one in all these lakes that can be called good. ... Above all, it has one singular property, namely, that all sorts of sauces spoil it, so that it is always ate either boiled or broiled, without any manner of seasoning."

BARON LA HONTAN, who accompanied Cadillac. 1688.

"... the most luxurious delicacy that swims the waters.
... I declare to you that I have never tasted anything of the kind half so exquisite. If the Roman Apicius had lived in these later days, he would certainly have made a voyage to Lake Huron to breakfast on the whitefish of St. Mary's River."

ANNA BROWNELL JAMESON. *Winter Studies and Summer Rambles.* 1839.

"... he who tastes it once, will thenceforth be unable to relish that of any other fish."

DANIEL DRAKE. *The Northern Lakes.* 1842.

"All friends of good living by tureen and dish,
    Concur in exalting this prince of a fish;
    So fine in a platter, so tempting a fry'
    So rich on a gridiron, so sweet in a pie;
    That even before it the salmon must fail,
    And that mighty boone-boucha, of the land-beaver's tail."

HENRY SCHOOLCRAFT. 1843.

"No human being ever wearied of good, fresh northern whitefish, no human being was ever made ill by eating too much of it."

U. P. HENDRICK. *The Land of the Crooked Tree.* 1948.

"Lake Whitefish, is a gift of the gods. It is not a beautiful fish, but it is among the most delicious on earth. ... Smoked, salted, boiled, baked, fried — there is nothing, simply nothing, quite like it!"

WILLIAM ASHWORTH. *The Late Great Lakes.* 1987.

Wolverine

"There is no authentic record of a wolverine ever being seen or killed in the state."

Michigan State Game Biologist F.W. STUEWER. *National Geographic.* March 1952.

"(A wolverine) ... is made up of a rather misfit collection of cast-off or leftover parts from other animals. Take the ears of a raccoon, the head of a small dog, ... the feet of a bear, (and) the legs of a badger. ..."

TOM OPRE, *Detroit Free Press* Outdoor Writer, quoting from an old, unnamed hunting magazine.

"The wolverine is not cute and cuddly. ... It has earned a reputation as a vicious, ugly glutton."

GARY W. BARFKNECHT. *Unexplained Michigan Mysteries.* 1993.

Wolves

"Northern Michigan was, and still is, one of the favorite resorts of the timber-wolf, owing to the dense forests and the abundance of deer and rabbits. Here I have shot a few and trapped or poisoned a dozen or so about the camp. ... they number thousands about Lake Superior."

GEORGE SHIRAS. *National Geographic.* August 1924.

Fishing

"In order to spear trout under the ice, holes being first cut two yards in circumference, cabins of about two feet in height are built over them of small branches and trees; and these are covered with skins as wholly to exclude the light. A spear head of iron is fastened on a pole of about ten feet in length. This instrument is lowered into the water; and the fisherman, lying on his belly, with his head under the cabin or cover, and therefore over the hole, lets down the figure of a fish in wood and filled with lead."

ALEXANDER HENRY. 1760s.

"I wish again
To fish again
In Michigan again"

DOUGLAS MALLOCH, Michigan poet. 1920s.

"I personally don't happen to care a whoop for bass fishing or bass; in fact I loathe it and them, but I have no quarrel with the queer people who do, only sort of bewildered pity."

JOHN VOELKER. *Trout Madness.* 1960.

"The smelt dipper is an all-around athlete — a combination of wrestler, adagio dancer, weightlifter — and player of blindman's-bluff. At times he becomes a swimmer."

KENDRICK KIMBALL. *Motor News.* April 1963.

Flora

General

"The roads were the best we had travelled since we left New York State. We passed through a wilderness of flowers; trailing roses, enormous white convolvulus, scarlet lilies, and ground ivy, with many other, being added to those we had before seen. Milton must have travelled through Michigan before he wrote the garden parts of 'Paradise Lost.'"

HARRIET MARTINEAU, British travel writer. 1834.

"The wild flowers of Michigan deserve a poet of their own."

CAROLINE KIRKLAND. *A New Home — Who'll Follow?* 1836.

"The forests are the greatest curiosity of the country — they are grand. You cannot conceive the majesty (if I may use the word) of the trees, some of which seem 'old as Time.'"

HANNAH COCHRANE, an early settler in Vermontville. 1838.

"The region was in one sense, wild, though it offered a picture that was not without some of the strongest and most pleasing features of civilizations. ... Although wooded, it was not as the American forest is wont to grow, with tall, straight trees towering toward the light, but with intervals between the low oaks that were scattered profusely over the view, and with much of that air of negligence that one is apt to see in grounds where art is made to assume the character of nature."

JAMES FENIMORE COOPER. *Oak Openings,* or the *Bee Hunter.* 1848. A description of the forests in southwestern Michigan.

"Most of the forests of Michigan south of Saginaw Bay died in a sacrificial manner — they were cut down and the logs burned to make room for fields."

CHARLES DAVIS. *Reading in Geography of Michigan.* 1964.

"During the month of August, the wilds of northern Michigan are lush with thimbleberries, blackberries, wild strawberries, gooseberries, dingleberries, hackberries, elderberries, whortleberries, boysenberries and blueberries. There are chokecherries, wild plums, green apples and peaches. There is wintergreen to sweeten the palate. And if there is anything of the gourmet about you, I have it on good authority that milkweed root is not to be excelled for sheer delicacy of flavor; unless, perhaps you find yourself in some gentle swale where cattail shoots may be gathered. The woods abound with wild goodies, and no man need go hungry. Not unless he runs out of cheese and crackers."

JOHN MACISAAC. *Half the Fun Was Getting There.* 1968.

Jack Pines

"To be sure, they are not the things of woodland architecture that might be desired. But like the cactus of Arizona or the sagebrush of Nevada, they are symbolic. They struggle on untiringly through the years, stunted and emaciated, waging a triumphal challenge. A futile life, but certainly proven survivors of the fittest."

HAZEL GIRARD. *Blow for Batten's Crossing.* 1979.

Skunk Cabbage

"Skunk cabbages! A thousand sonnets died in that misnomer."

HENRY SEIDEL CANBY. Date unknown

Great Lakes

General

See also *Ships and Shipping*

"I do not know why the name 'lakes' has been given to these watery deeps of such vast extent. ... I think it important, and even necessary for the satisfaction of inquiring minds, to explain what reasons there may have been for dividing this single lake into five parts; I call it one only, because it is indisputable that it is one and the same body of water, communicating with and flowing from one to the other."

CADILLAC, founder of Detroit. 1716.

"There is something in the character of these basins of water, and in the multitude of them, which imparts a charm to this region, altogether unrivalled."

C. COLTON. *Tour of the American Lakes.* 1833.

"I have seen the storm of the Channel, those of the Ocean, the squalls off the banks of Newfoundland, those on the coasts of America, and the hurricanes of the Gulf of Mexico. No where have I witnessed the fury of the elements comparable to that found on this fresh water sea."

FRANCIS COUNT DE CASTELAU. 1842.

"It is difficult for the imagination adequately to conceive the extent of the fresh-water oceans."

FRANCES PARKMAN. *The Conspiracy of Pontiac.* 1851.

"For in their interflowing aggregate, those grand fresh-water seas of ours, — Erie, and Ontario, and Huron, and Superior, and Michigan, — possess an ocean-like expansiveness, with many of the ocean's noblest traits; with many of its rimmed varieties of races and of climes. They are swept by Borean and dismasting blasts as direful as any that lash the salted wave; they know what shipwrecks are, for out of sight of land, however inland, they have drowned full many a midnight ship with all its shrieking crew."

HERMAN MELVILLE. *Moby Dick.* 1851.

"If people in England had any idea of the lovely scenery and delightful climate of the American lakes, they would not confine their yachting to European waters."

LAURENCE OLIPHANT, Canadian Superintendent of Indian Affairs. 1854.

"There is a sublimity about these vast fresh-water seas which is hardly exceeded by the ocean itself."

BELA HUBBBARD. *Memorials of a Half-Century in Michigan and the Lakes Region.* 1887.

"My memory in the distance sees the sails glistening white,
Or the gleam of many torchlights upon the bay at night,
The shores so white and rocky and the fine shifting sand,
And, oh, I'm longing — longing — for the bays of Michigan."

From the poem "Longing," by LIZZIE LANGWORTHY CONNINE. 1890s.

"The sentiment of the human heart which experiences pleasure in the sublime and the beautiful in nature, can find on the waters of the Great Lakes and in their environment a wealth of enjoyment that is offered nowhere else on the globe."

JOHN MANSFIELD. *History of the Great Lakes.* 1899.

"... the greatest pleasure-grounds in the world."

JAMES OLIVER CURWOOD. *The Great Lakes.* 1909.

"The American Mediterranean."

ANDREW H. BROWN. *National Geographic.* March 1952.

"It is quite easy to simulate the joys of yacht racing in your own home. All you have to do is stand in a very cold shower and tear up twenty-dollar bills."

A Great Lakes yachtsman. 1972.

"Neither the Americans who dwell along the seaboards nor those who hail from the inland reaches of plains and mountains can understand the vastness of the Great Lakes. Here, where the high walls of water stretch in lonesome grandeur to the horizon, only seeing is believing."

WILLIAM RATIGAN. *Great Lakes Shipwrecks and Survivals.* 1977.

"It is an old joke, and a true one, on the Great Lakes that salt-water sailors often become seasick on what they have been known to call, disparagingly, our inland ponds, before close acquaintance turns them green in the face and forces a respectful bow over the rail."

WILLIAM RATIGAN. *Great Lakes Shipwrecks and Survivals.* 1977.

"The waters of the upper Lakes are indeed summertime playgrounds, but the season is from the Fourth of July to Labor Day. The rest of the year they are no place for a picnic, and even during the vacation months they must be treated with uninterrupted respect by the summertime sailor who wants to enjoy another season."

WILLIAM RATIGAN. *Great Lakes Shipwrecks and Survivals.* 1977.

"There are two ironies about the Great Lakes: first, that the people who have become most dependent upon them have misused them the most; and second, that despite our abuse of them the lakes remain as wondrous as they must have seemed to ... the first European to see them. ..."

JOHN ROUSMANIERE. *The Enduring Great Lakes.* 1979.

"Few fully comprehend the awesome size of what has been called the world's 'eighth sea' or the dangers faced by those who sail upon these often cruel and bellicose waters."

ROBERT J. HEMMING. *Gales of November: The Sinking of the Edmund Fitzgerald.* 1981.

"... the Great Lakes have a voracious appetite for ships and sailors."

JACK PARKER. *Shipwrecks of Lake Huron.* 1986.

"Singly each lake is an inland sea in itself, larger, more dangerous and with dirtier weather than many a sea better known in song and story."

FRANK BARCUS. *Freshwater Fury.* 1986.

"The Great Lakes need ask no odds of any sea on earth when it comes to staging a hell-roaring storm in early winter."

FRANK BARCUS. *Freshwater Fury.* 1986

"The misunderstanding runs very deep, as deep as the name itself: Great Lakes. In no conventional sense are these lakes. ... they are something else, something separate and unique and wonderful."

WILLIAM ASHWORTH. *The Late Great Lakes*. 1987.

"I don't understand why people are afraid to sail the Great Lakes. No matter where you are on the lakes you're no farther than 1,300 feet from land. It may be straight down but it's land."

JOHN McMURRAY, meteorologist and Great Lakes sailor. 1991.

Lake Erie

"... an odorous, slime-covered grave-yard."

ALAN EDMONDS. *MacLean's Magazine*. August 20, 1965.

"The Dead Sea."

Newsweek. April 12, 1965.

"Even a line squall on treacherous Erie seems to scoop this shallowest of the Great Lakes from its muddy bottom and hurl it at the sky."

WILLIAM RATIGAN. *Great Lakes Shipwrecks and Survivals*. 1977.

"... it is, Lake Erie the shallowest of all the Great Lakes, that stabs the sailor's heart with icy fear. For even on a beautiful summer day, when the surface appears as hard and polished as a spacious mirror, a sudden squall can churn those shallow waters into a savage madness that can hammer and smash and suck the unprepared vessel below the maelstrom to later vomit bodies and bits of wreckage along its verdant shoreline."

ROBERT J. HEMMINGS. *Gales of November: The Sinking of the Edmund Fitzgerald*. 1981.

Lake Huron

"I love the purity of this water, and to float upon it; and look beneath at a bottom of sand, and shells, and pebbles, and see them as distinctly for twenty feet, as if there were no medium more dense than air between them and me."

THOMAS L. McKENNEY. *Sketches of a Tour of the Lakes*. 1826.

"The greatest fury of the wide Atlantic is mere mockery to Huron's maddest moods and roughest shapes. The most experienced mariner of the former has been filled with wonder, and stood aghast at the terrors of the later."

CALVIN COTTON. *Tour of the American Lakes, and Among the Indians of the Northwest Territory in 1830*.

"The Royal Geographer looking for the first time upon one of the mighty lakes on earth, upon the central waterway of what was to be the richest and busiest region in the world, wrote in his journal that he had found — squashes."

HARLAN HATCHER. *The Great Lakes*. 1944. Hatcher, commenting on Champlain's account of the discovery of the Great lakes.

"Lake Huron, the first Great Lake discovered, is the second largest, the third in the lake chain, the fourth most populated, and the last to come to the American mind."

Outdoor World. *The Great Lakes: North America's Inland Sea*. 1974.

"... deep and wide and cold and deadly."

BRUCE CATTON. *Michigan: A Bicentennial History.* 1976

"Lake Huron, the lake that swallowed eight big ore carriers in one single storm, is rougher, tougher and more violently ferocious than any other of our oceans."

JACK PARKER. *Shipwrecks of Lake Huron.* 1986.

"Lake Huron, ... where 40% of all lake ships come to die."

JACK PARKER. *Shipwrecks of Lake Huron.* 1986.

Lake Michigan

"The Man-Devouring Lake."

Chippewa name for Lake Michigan.

"Would to heaven, that I could forever forget Lake Michigan! Her envious waves have, recently, buried a youth of noble promise."

ESTIVICK EVANS. *A Predestrious Tour of Four Thousand Miles, Through the Western States and Territories, During the Winter and Spring of 1818.*

"To Lake Michigan ... sailing masters pay the utmost respect, not only because of this Lake's long history of sudden disaster, but because of the prevailing winds that can sweep its length to roll up backbreaking seas, the scarcity of natural harbors ... and the crowning fact that it is the trickiest of the Lakes to keep a course on due to currents caused by a flow around the Straits of Mackinac when the wind shifts."

WILLIAM RATIGAN. *Great Lakes Shipwrecks and Survivals.* 1977.

Lake Superior

"The savages revere this lake as a divinity."

FATHER ALLOUEZ. 1665.

"The water was as pure and transparent as air, and my canoe seemed as if hung, suspended in that element. It was impossible to look attentively through this liquid medium at the rocks below without finding before many minutes were elapsed, your head swim, and your eyes no longer able to behold the dazzling view."

JONATHON CARVER, an early traveler on the lake. 1778.

"There is not perhaps on the globe a body of water so pure and so light as that of Lake Superior. It appears conscious of its innate excellence: the innumerable tainted streams which pour into it are forced to creep merely along the beach without once being able to make an impression on its unstained bosom."

JOHN JOHNSTON. *An Account of Lake Superior, 1792-1807.*

"This lake is remarkable for the pure and pellucid appearance of its water. The fish in it can be seen swimming at a great depth; and the vessels upon it seem to move in the air."

ESTIVICK EVANS. *A Predestrious Tour of Four Thousand Miles, Through the Western States, During the Winter and Spring of 1818.*

"The lake is one of the most boisterous in the world. I have seen it when our sails would not flop and in fifteen minutes blowing a gale and the seas in a few moments more running as high as a house."

From a letter by PHILO M. EVERETT, written while on a trip to Keweenaw. 1845.

"The waters of this magnificent lake are marvelously clear, and even at midsummer are exceedingly cold. In passing along its rocky shore in my frail canoe, I have often been alarmed at the sight of a sunken boulder, which I fancied must be near the top, and on further investigation have found myself to upwards of twenty feet from the danger of concussion; and I have frequently lowered a white rag to the depth of one hundred feet, and been able to discern it every fold and stain.

... the climate of Lake Superior at midsummer is delightful beyond compare; and the air is soft and bracing at the same time. A healthier region does not exist on the earth, I verily believe, and this assertion is corroborated by the well known fact that inhabitants usually live to an advanced age, in spite of their many hardships."

CHARLES LANMAN. *A Summer in the Wilderness: Embracing a Canoe Voyage Up the Mississippi and Around Lake Superior.* 1847.

"He who, for the first time, lifts his eyes upon this expanse, is amazed and delighted at its magnitude. Vastness is the term by which it is, more than any other, described."

HENRY SCHOOLCRAFT. 1851.

"The famous purity of the water of this region is indeed one of the most extraordinary things to be noticed here. So great is this purity; so entirely free is the water of the streams and springs from earthly or foreign matter of any kind, that the daguerrotypist finds it better for his purpose than the best distilled water of the chemist."

ROBERT E. CLARKE. *Harpers Monthly.* March 1853.

"... those who have never seen Superior get an inadequate even inaccurate idea, by hearing it spoken of as a 'lake,' and to those who have sailed over its vast extent the word sounds ludicrous."

REVEREND GEORGE GRANT, the diarist of an 1872 expedition on the lake.

"... thoughts of an open boat on Lake Superior will make the hardiest of men shiver."

CHARLES DAVIS, lightkeeper at Copper Harbor. 1891.

"... magnificent belittlers of the grandest of Nature's achievements, call it a lake yet which, were it in Europe, would have become one of the seas of the world, paraded by fleets of war and dividing empires."

JULIAN RALPH. 1899.

"Great Cold Lake in an Iron Collar."

STEWART HOLBROCK. *Iron Brew.* 1939. Holbrock is alluding to the vast iron deposits that ring the lake.

"Nowhere in the world, probably has geology more of an appeal, to the causal traveler than around Lake Superior. ... Almost from the moment of approaching it the traveler realizes that here is a great rock basin not filled to the top with water."

GRACE NUTE. *Lake Superior.* 1944.

"Lake Superior is the big, bad wolf of the Great Lakes."

JOSEPH E. and ESTELLE BAYLISS. *Rivers of Destiny.* 1955.

"... beautiful, empty, glittering, cold and brooding, gull-swept and impersonal; always there, always the same — there for the grateful and ungrateful, there for the bastards and angels."

JOHN VOELKER. *Anatomy of a Murder.* 1958.

"... those who know the lake never really trust it."

Outdoor World. *The Great Lakes: North America's Inland Sea.* 1974.

"Depending on the season, Lake Superior has two temperatures — solid ice and melted ice."

WILLIAM RATIGAN. *Great Lakes Shipwrecks and Survivals.* 1977.

"To say that Lake Superior is the greatest of the Great Lakes is to say much, but it draws no picture of the vastness of this haughty queen of fresh water who has a copper crown, the iron hills for a footstool and the coldest blue eyes in creation."

WILLIAM RATIGAN. *Great Lakes Shipwrecks and Survivals.* 1977.

"Lake Superior is among the cruelest of the cruel seas anywhere."

LESLIE ARNDT. *The Bay County Story.* 1982.

"The industrial supremacy of the United States among nations is due wholly to the purity, abundance, cheapness of mining and low rate of transportation of Lake Superior ores."

RALPH D. WILLIAMS. *The Honorable Peter White.* 1986.

"Learned men with no learning call it a lake."

WILLIAM ASHWORTH. *The Late Great Lake.* 1987.

Inland Lakes

Barron Lake

"If I had three wishes, three wishes I'd wish: To be young, unemployed, and at Barron Lake, Mich."

RING LARDNER. An undated couplet from the Bentley Library at the University of Michigan.

Burt Lake

"... one of the prettiest lakes ever looked upon by a tourist."

Various sources, the most recent of which is *They Left Their Marks* by JOHN S. BURT. 1985.

Crystal Lake

"Its clearness, purity, pellucid quality, its almost atmospheric transparency, could be expressed by no other word than 'crystal.'"

JOHN HOWARD. *The Story of Frankfort.* 1930.

"Crystal Lake is a noble body of water. ... It is surrounded by low green hills, and when the sun is out its color is a breathtaking, incredible, picture-postcard blue; spring-fed, it is deep and cold, and only the hardiest would care to swim in it at any time except midsummer, but when the weather is warm to go into this water is like dipping into the fountain of youth."

BRUCE CATTON. *Waiting for the Morning Train.* 1972.

Glen Lake

"Among the five most beautiful lakes in the world."

National Geographic. April 1934.

Higgins Lake

"The water is so clear that a nickel can be seen at a depth of forty feet, and it has the peculiarity of always showing at least four distinct colors on the surface, dark purple, blue and shades of green."

Michigan Central Railroad. *The Fairy Isle of Mackinac.* 1888.

Houghton Lake

"... blue water for blue collars. ... when Traverse City was celebrating its first Hudson's, construction began on Houghton Lake's first Kmart."

NEAL RUBIN. *Detroit Free Press Magazine.* September 6, 1992.

"The four townships that surround Houghton Lake look like Traverse City before Izod shirts."

NEAL RUBIN. *Detroit Free Press.* July 7, 1992.

Lake St. Clair

"The strait, thirty leagues long, is a league wide almost everywhere except in the middle portion. Here it widens out, forming a round lake ten leagues in diameter. We named it Lake St. Clair since we crossed it in the day of the saint."

FATHER LOUIS HENNEPIN. 1683.

"The centre of the lake presents a beautiful and enchanting looming up of the shores, as the sailors call it, in all directions; and the marginal forests, broken every here and there, by the indentations of the coast, seem to hang suspended in the horizon, between the sea and the heavens, and play and dance before the eye, in a sort of fairy vision."

C. COLTON. *Tour of the American Lakes.* 1833.

Lake Gogebic

"It is the gem of the northland; a lake once seen never to be forgotten. So quiet and unmolested, so fair and fresh, so guarded by trees and low-growing bushes is it that one looking for the first time, from some distant height, upon the placid surface imagines he sees a diamond lodged in an emerald setting."

H. F. WHITCOMB, General Manager, Milwaukee, Lake Shore & Western Railway. 1886.

Torch Lake

"Torch Lake has driven writers to poetic exhaustion when trying to describe its beauty."

GLEN RUGGLES. *Michigan History Magazine.* January/February 1979.

"... the most appealing pond in Michigan."

SONNY ELIOT. *Michigan Living.* September 1988.

Walloon Lake

"The area is still beautiful, green and hilly with a vernal juiciness that reminds one of the Lake Country in England. But it's hard to identify the landscape with the woods, swamps and rivers where Nick Adams played Injun, and endured the rites of passage that Hemingway wrote so cleanly about. Not, anyway, when you see a million-dollar condominium peeking through the woods like some sort of fey Rotarian Xanadu."

JIM HARRISON. *Just Before Dark.* 1977.

Islands

Beaver Island

"During the winter months more decks of cards are worn out on Beaver Island than any other similiar island in the world."

Republic-News and St. Ignace Enterprise. February 23, 1923.

"All conditions taken into consideration, getting mail to Beaver Island the year around is probably one of the most difficult assignments the postal department has to contend with."

Detroit News. 1926.

"Beaver Island can be one of the quietest places in the world."

ELA JOHNSON. *The Faces of the Great Lakes.* 1977.

"There are no peaks standing out as distinct landmarks because Beaver Island was not thrust up from the depths of the sea like the lava cones of Hawaii; instead it is a remnant of the withdrawal of the last ice age which left it like a stranded toy in a half drained bath tub."

HENRY L. HILL. Tales From the Other End of the Island. 1991.

"If you live to shop, you'll have a life expectancy of less than three hours (on Beaver Island)."

TOM POWERS. *More Natural Michigan.* 1992.

Belle Isle

"In the middle of the strait and about two miles above the city, is a superb island. I could have wished they had called it by another name than Hog Island."

THOMAS L. McKENNEY. *Sketches of a Tour to the Lakes. 1826.* Before being named Belle Isle in 1845, the island had several names including Hog.

"To the south is the Detroit River and the beautiful green isle of Belle Isle where on any summer evening it is said you can find three thousand empty soft-drink bottles, and almost as many less attractive objects."

HAROLD LIVINGSTONE. *The Detroiters.* 1958.

Drummond Island

"Pigeons and ducks at certain seasons are so plentiful that it is said (I do not vouch for the fact) that you only have to fire up the chimney and a couple of ducks will fall into the pot."

JOHN J. BIGSBY, Secretary of the British Boundary Commission. 1823.

"It is not possible for anything to be more sterile than is Drummond's island. It is the picture of barrenness. Covered with limestone, there is scarcely upon its elevations a foot of ground, except here and there, and around its shores, out of which vegetation can grow."

THOMAS L. McKENNEY. *Sketches of a Tour of the Lakes.* 1826.

"It's got everything on it: unrivaled scenery, rocks, uncompromising challenge, rocks, carpetlike fairways and greens, an away-from-it all feeling, rocks.

... the best golf course in the world you can't get to."

RICK SYLVAIN. *Michigan Living*. March 1991. Description of "The Rock" golf course on Drummond Island.

Grand Island

"Grand Island affords one of the most beautiful and sheltered harbors in the world."

J. W. FOSTER and J. D. WHITNEY. *Report on the Geology of the Lake Superior District*. 1851.

"... there is no other Island which could have the Pictured Rocks for an approach, and not suffer in comparison."

BEATRICE H. CASTLE. *The Grand Island Story*. 1974.

"Nature has made Grand Island one of the most beautiful spots on the world."

U.S. Dept. of Agriculture, Forest Service brochure. circa 1980.

Isle Royale

"Gold, rubies, and precious stones are found (there) in abundance."

ETIENNE BRULE, the first European to visit Michigan. 1634.

"This must be the North Pole."

November 4, 1885, diary entry by Isle Royale lighthouse keeper JOHN MALONE.

"The proposal to conserve it as a national park is worthy of its character."

BELA HUBBARD. *Memorials of a Half-Century in Michigan and the Lakes Region*. 1887.

"... it seemed to me the acme of romance, as remote and thrilling as Spitzbergen or Sanzibar."

WEBB WALDRON. *We Explore the Great Lakes*. 1923.

"... forged in ancient fires and machined to beauty by the sun, wind and waves of a million years. ..."

FRED DUSTIN. *Detroit News*. September 8, 1929.

"Isle Royale and its romance! Blah! It's a hunk of mud."

From the diary of DOROTHY McQUOWN, a school teacher on the island in the winter of 1932-33.

"... one of nature's rarest sanctuaries in all of this New World."

SENATOR ARTHUR VANDENBERG. *Ann Arbor News*. August 27, 1946.

"It is an Enchanted Isle where one may summon the spirits of the past in mental vision; where the rocks personify strength;

the cold waters, depth; the forests, wilderness; the skies, with their mysterious aurora and fleeting mirage, mystery."

FRED DUSTIN. *Michigan History Magazine.* March 1957.

... in geological time, man's involvement with the island is like a fistful of sand on a wide beach. The plants and animals, trees and rocks, wind and waves, will own Isle Royale just as they always have."

PETER OIKARINEN. *Island Folk: The People of Isle Royale.* 1979.

"... Isle Royale demands a hardy species of visitor."

JOHN L. ELIOT. *National Geographic.* April 1985.

"... one of the premier wilderness experiences of the National Park System."

JOHN L. ELIOT. *National Geographic.* April 1985.

"Days are measured by footsteps, not by alarm clocks or 10 o'clock news."

CLAIRE BUHL. *Travel Holiday.* July 1987.

""... the ultimate Midwestern wilderness experience. ..."

MARY and DON HUNT. *Hunt's Highlights of Michigan.* 1991.

TOM POWERS

Mackinac Island

See also *Architecture* (Grand Hotel), *Landmarks* (Straits of Mackinac), *Military Forts* (Fort Mackinac), and *Tourism*

"Gibralter of the North West."

SAMUEL R. BROWN. *The Western Gazetteer*. 1817.

"Nothing can present a more picturesque or refreshing spectacle to the traveller, wearied with the lifeless monotony of a canoe voyage through Lake Huron, than the first sight of the island of Michilimackinac, which rises from the watery horizon in lofty bluffs imprinting a rugged outline along the sky."

HENRY SCHOOLCRAFT. 1820.

"Nothing can exceed the beauty of this island. ... If the poetic muses are ever to have a new Parnassus in America, they should inevitably fix on Michilimackinac. Hygeia, too, should place her temple here; for it has one of the purest, driest, clearest, and most healthful atmospheres."

HENRY SCHOOLCRAFT. 1820.

"Mackinac is worth seeing. I think it by no means improbable, especially should steamboats extend their route to it, that it will become a place of fashionable resort for the summer, ... But in winter I would prefer not to be here; and that would form an exception, as to temperature, at least seven months out of the twelve."

THOMAS L. McKENNEY. *Sketches of a Tour of the Lakes*. 1826.

"These were the palmy days of Mackinac. It was no unusual thing to see a hundred or more canoes of Indians at once approaching the island, laden with their articles of traffic; and if to these was added the squadron of large Mackinac boats constantly arriving from the outposts with furs, peltries and buffalo robes collected by distant traders, some idea may be formed of the extensive operations and the important position of the American Fur Company, as well as of the vast circle of human beings either immediately or remotely connected with it."

MRS. JOHN KINZIE. 1830.

"It is so healthy here, that a person has to get off the island to die."

A soldier stationed on the island. 1830.

"Isle of the Blessed."

HENRY SCHOOLCRAFT. 1830s.

"The town of Mackina is composed entirely of one story log-houses, roofed with cedar bark; it has a dilapidated appearance, and is, in fact, fast going to decay. ... Certainly I have never seen a place which presented as many picturesque objects. ..."

CHANDLER GILMAN. *Life on the Lakes*. 1836.

"... the wildest and tenderest little piece of beauty that I have yet seen on God's earth."

HARRIET MARTINEAU. A famous British author on a trip to America in 1837.

"It has the appearance of a fairy isle floating on the water, which is so pure and transparent that you can see down to almost any depth; and the air above is as pure as the water, so that you feel invigorated as you breath it.

I inquired ... (of an islander) if people live to a good old age on the island; his reply was quite American. 'I guess they do; if people want to die, they can't die here — they're obliged to go elsewhere.' "

From the 1837 diary of CAPTAIN MARRYAT, a popular British author.

"The place is the picture of an ancient Canadian settlement, the little houses in Canadian style, some of them log, with roofs thatched with bark, the picket-fences of rough sharpened stakes that surround them all, the canoes and Indian huts on the shore give them a wild and picturesque air."

FRANCIS PARKMAN, historian. 1845.

"I spoke in one of my former letters of the manifest fate of Mackinaw, which is to be a watering place. I cannot see how it is to escape this destiny. People already begin to repair to it for health and refreshment from the southern borders of Lake Michigan. Its climate during the summer months is delightful; there is no air more pure and elastic, and the winds of the south and southwest, which are so hot on the prairies, arrive here tempered to a grateful coolness by the waters over which they have swept. The nights are always, in the hottest season, agreeably cool, and the health of the place is proverbial. The world has not many islands so beautiful as Mackinaw."

WILLIAM CULLEN BRYANT, in a letter dated August 20, 1846.

"It is indeed one of the most unique and delightful places in the world. ... I first approached it from the north, on a mild and hazy afternoon. I looked upon it in perfect silence, fearing that even the beating of my heart would dispel what I thought to a mere illusion."

CHARLES LANMAN. *A Summer in the Wilderness: Embracing a Canoe Voyage Up the Mississippi and Around Lake Superior.* 1847.

"Mackinaw is at the present moment crowded with strangers; attracted by the cool healthful climate and the extreme beauty of the place. We were packed for the night almost as closely as the Potawot-tamis, whose lodges were on the beach before us. Parlors and garrots were turned into sleeping-rooms; beds were made on floors and in passages, and double-bedded rooms were made to receive four beds. It is no difficult feat to sleep at Mackinaw, even in an August night, and we soon forgot, in a refreshing slumber, the narrowness of our quarters."

WILLIAM CULLEN BRYANT. *Letters of a Traveller.* 1850.

"As a place of resort during the summer months, there can be none more desirable — none possessing more attractive features and health-restoring influences, than this Island of Mackinaw."

New York Weekly Tribune. July 9, 1853.

"For a fresh, bracing, and delightful air, probably the States do not afford a pleasanter spot than Mackinac."

ROBERT E. CLARKE. *Harpers Monthly.* March 1853.

"Ten times more liquor is drunk in Mackinac than any other town of the same population."

JAMES JESSE STRANG. *Ancient and Modern Michilimackinac.* 1854.

"... a barren pile of limestone.
The attempt to make Mackinac a fashionable resort, never very successful, must fail entirely on the completion of the Sault Ste. Marie Canal, and the opening of the Lake Superior country to visitors, seeking summer retreats."

JAMES JESSE STRANG. *Ancient and Modern Michilimackinac.* 1854. Mr. Strang, who was the leader of a group of Mormons on Beaver Island, did not like the idea of a large number of gentiles on Mackinac Island and was probably trying to discourage people from visiting the place.

"I have never breathed such air before; and this must be some that was clear out of Eden, and did not get cursed."

HORACE MANN, in a letter written in 1857.

"The Island of Mackinac, ... already visited for its picturesque beauty, may, probably, become the future Newport, of the north-western states."

The New World in 1859: Being the United States and Canada.

"Ye inhabitants of warm latitudes who pant in cities for a breath of cool air, fly to this isle of comfort. Ye invalid, this is the place in which to renovate your shattered constitution."

J. DISTURNELL. *The Great Lakes or Inland Seas of America.* 1868.

"That so much of the island of Mackinac, lying in the Straits of Mackinac within the county of Mackinac, in the State of Michigan, as is now held by the United States under military reservation or otherwise ... hereby is reserved and withdrawn from settlement, occupancy or sale under the laws of the United States, and dedicated and set apart as a national park, or grounds, for health, comfort and pleasure, for the benefit and enjoyment of the people."

SENATOR THOMAS W. FERRY, on the floor of the U.S. Senate in 1873. Ferry's proposal was accepted in 1875 and the island became America's second national park. In 1895 the island was transferred to the State of Michigan.

"The natural scenery of the island of Mackinac is unsurpassed. Nature seems to have exhausted herself in the clustered objects of interest which every-where meet the eye."

REV. J. A. VAN FLEET. *Old and New Mackinac.* 1874.

"There is scarcely a spot in all the new world that more nearly unites in itself all

TOM POWERS

the glories and beauties and advantages that constitute a perfect tourist's paradise."

Michigan Central Railroad. 1888.

"Too much tranquility has a reaction. Mackinac Island will be obligated to let the automobile in, or build a factory or a trolley line or something or, I am afraid, it will lose its clientele."

WEBB WALDRON. *We Explore the Great Lakes.* 1923.

"If DDT drives the flies and the mosquitoes from Mackinac as St. Patrick drove the snakes from Ireland, it will prove a blessing indeed."

ARTHUR W. STACE. Tourist & Resort Advisory Committee. 1945.

"Michilimackinac is a stumbling block for anyone who writes or talks about Michigan. There are innumerable ways to spell it, there is argument over its meaning, and there is no logic whatever to its pronunciation; on top of which, it does not stay put properly as a historic place should."

BRUCE CATTON. *Michigan: A Bicentennial History.* 1976.

"Aside from the hotel trade, the business that seems most successful on Mackinac is that of making fudge. Never are the streets not scented with chocolate."

MIMI ELDER. *Gourmet Magazine.* June 1989.

"... one of the last great Victorian resorts in America, a smaller — and purer — version of Martha's Vineyard. ..."

EDMUND WHITE. *House & Garden.* June 1990.

"Michigan's ivory tower, our enchanted attic, our version of Camelot."

DORIS SCHARFENBERG. *Long Blue Edge of Summer.* 1992.

South Manitou Island

"I return to South Manitou to recapture that feeling of peace — not to mention the fact that the harbor's cold, clear water provides the best swimming in the universe."

EDWARD HOOGTERP. *Flint Journal.* May 10, 1992.

Literature

"... sober honesty compels the admission that authors — upper case authors — are about as rare in Michigan as the 'skunk bear' ever was and that the flowering of literary Michigan is still in the future.

Michigan has put the world on automobile wheels, (but) Michigan novelists are still jogging along in one-hoss shays."

ARNOLD MULDER. *Saturday Review of Literature.* March 4, 1939.

"I'd rather flunk my Wasserman test
Than read a poem by Eddie Guest."

DOROTHY PARKER. Date unknown but thought to be circa 1940.

"Lake Superior has produced no piece of art of greater genius than Hiawatha. When that is said, it is obvious that nothing of immortal worth in poetry, prose, sculpture, painting or music has come from the great lake and its setting."

GRACE NUTE. *Lake Superior.* 1944.

"... (Elmore) Leonard's nine Detroit books form as good a portrait of life in this city during the past 20 years — its unwritten codes and attitudes, its views of the world, its excesses and eccentricities — as we'll have."

NEELY TUCKER. *Detroit Free Press Magazine.* March 29, 1992.

Lumbering Era

"For all its handicaps, the lumber industry in Michigan was basically an industry that grew great in a time when it could hardly do anything else."

BRUCE CATTON, describing lumbering during the 1800s. *Michigan: A Bicentennial History*. 1976.

"Two out of every three pine trees that came crashing to the ground in Michigan's Lower Peninsula in the nineteenth century ended up in Saginaw, or Bay City, or Muskegon."

A description of the lumbering era during the 1800s by JEREMY KILAR. *Michigan's Lumbertowns*. 1990.

"We'll never cut all this pine if we log it until hell freezes."

Observation of one of the first Maine lumberjacks to arrive in Michigan during the 1840s. The trees, however, were all but gone by 1900.

"... whosoever holds good pine lands in Michigan ten years from now, that have been purchased at the present rates, will have the most valuable property in the country."

GEORGE P. TITUS of New York. 1850.

"Going into the pineries is like going to war."

An unknown logger commenting on the dangerous life of a lumberjack. 1850s.

"In dollar value, Michigan's 'green gold' out valued California's 'yellow gold' by more than a billion dollars.

STAN BERRIMAN, telling the worth of timber that was harvested in Michigan from 1847-1899. *Upper Tittabawasse River Boom Towns*. 1977.

"If all the lumber cut in Michigan during the white pine lumbering era (1860-1900) would provide enough boards for a solid row of out-houses around the world, as some writers stated, then the amount of whiskey consumed by lumberjacks, tough guys, drummers, and plain drunks during the same period would have made another set of Great Lakes bubbling over with pure whiskey."

ROY L. DODGE. *Ticket to Hell: A Saga of Michigan's Bad Men*. 1975.

"The average lumberjack in the nineteenth century was reasonably content with just enough money to buy liquor, tobacco, women and lesser necessities."

ROBERT W. WELLS. *Daylight in the Swamp*. 1978.

"In one month alone in 1868, 1,694 tugs, 442 sailing sloops, 217 barges and 326 steamers passed through Third Street in Bay City."

HAROLD FOEHL. *The Story of Logging White Pine in the Saginaw Valley*. 1964.

"Forests were mowed like wheat."

ROBERT CONOT, describing Michigan during the 1870s. *American Odyssey*. 1974

"The lusty lumberjacks left behind them legends, most of them made up from sheer boredom and the poverty of reality. More importantly, they left behind great vulgar cut-over areas where only stumps and rotting tops and underbrush remained; a kind of early-stage, low-grade Nagasaki, a quality of destruction not yet much advanced by technology."

CURTIS K. SLADTFIELD. *From the Land and Back.* 1972.

"(During the 1880s) the only toiletries north of Saginaw were moustache wax and alkali soap."

RUSSELL McKEE. *Audubon Magazine.* March 1988.

"Daily dress was heavy boots, heavy wool pants, itchy shirts, and thick wool jackets of the type that weigh ten pounds dry, forty wet. All this clothing came in one size: wrong."

RUSSELL MCKEE, describing the life of a lumberjack during the 1880s. *Audubon Magazine.* March 1988

"The only language the stumps understood in Upper Michigan is the Finnish language."

J. H. JASBERG, a Finnish colonizing agent, on the number of Finnish lumberjacks in the U.P. in the late 1800s.

"It was said a Jack was no good unless he could chew tobacco, spit a yard and split a shingle."

Lumberjack life during the 1880s described by JOHN J. RIORDAN. *The Dark Peninsula.* 1976.

"Hard working, rough and ready, big hearted, generous, fraternal, impulsive, a hand for a friend, a foot for a foe, foolishly prodigal with his hard earned wealth, happy under very questionable conditions for joy, sensitive to the sorrows of others

more than his own, and faithful to his engagements where he is used with even moderate consideration and kindness.

If there is a dollar in the world that represents a man's life blood it is the dollar of the shanty boy (lumberjack)! If there is an honest dollar spent more foolishly than another, it is frequently the dollar of the shanty boy!

Yes! It is a life of toil, but also one of health. It is virtually kill or cure."

JOHN W. FITZMAURICE. *The Shanty Boy.* 1889.

"One can ride through the heart of the pine country from Manistee on the west to Saginaw on the east, and see ... miles upon miles of stumps. ..."

PROFESSOR A. A. CROZIER. 1896.

"The finest white pine and hardwood forest in the world is now a man-made desert of fire blasted stumps and slashings."

An anonymous logger. 1900.

"Timber was gold to the Saginaw Valley."

STUART GROSS. *Indians, 'Jacks, and Pines.* 1962.

"If one is to understand the history of our state, its economic status, the location and growth of most of our cities and villages, and the large problems in land economy with which the people of Michigan are confronted, read the history of the depletion of the states forests."

BERT HUDGINS. *Michigan Geographic Backgrounds in the Development of the Commonwealth.* 1961.

"The state of Michigan had been ... developed by man's ability to turn forests into stacks of sawn boards faster than nature could produce forests in the first place."

BRUCE CATTON. *Waiting for the Morning Train.* 1972.

"The amount of virgin timber left in Michigan wouldn't cover Central Park."

JIM HARRISON. *Sundog.* 1984.

Michigan (General)

"This country, so temperate, so fertile, and so beautiful that it may justly be called the earthly paradise of North America. ..."

CADILLAC, founder of Detroit. 1702.

"... this is the finest part of all Canada; and really we can judge by appearances, nature seems to have denied it nothing which can contribute to make a country delightful: hills, meadows, fields, lofty forests, rivulets, fountains, rivers, and all of them so excellent in their kind and so happily blended as to equal the most romantic wishes."

PIERRE FRANCOIS XAVIER DE CHARLEVOIX, touring Canada as an agent for the king of France. 1720.

"A great part of the Territory is miserably poor, especially near Lakes Michigan and Erie. The districts, therefore, in which these fall will never contain sufficient number of inhabitants to entitle them to membership in the confederacy."

Future President JAMES MONROE, on a trip of Michigan Territory in 1787.

"The whole territory is a double frontier; the British are on one side, the savages on the other. Every individual house is a frontier."

From a memorandum sent to the president from a meeting in December 10, 1811, parties unknown.

"... the environs of Detroit excepted, the whole peninsula of Michigan lay in a state of nature."

JAMES FENIMORE COOPER, describing Michigan as it was in 1812. *The Oak Openings.* 1848.

"I have no hesitation to say that it would be to the advantage of the government to remove every inhabitant of the territory, pay for the improvements, and reduce them to ashes, leaving nothing but garrison posts. From my observation the territory appears to me not worth defending, and merely a den of Indians and Traitors."

GENERAL DUNCAN McARTHUR, Military Commander at Detroit. 1814.

"Taking the country altogether so far it has been explored, and to all appearances, together with the information received to the balance, it is so bad there would not be one acre out of one hundred, if there would be more than one thousand, that would in any case admit of cultivation."

EDWARD TIFFLIN, Surveyor General of the State of Ohio. 1815.

"It is impossible to look upon the present situation of Michigan and not be impressed. It is destined soon to emerge as a great, rich state. ... The future of Michigan appears to be certain, defined, fulled of promise and expansion."

ELKANAH WATSON, father of the Erie Canal, on a visit to Detroit. 1816.

"In traveling more than four thousand miles, in the western parts of the United States, I met no tract of country which, upon the whole, impressed my mind so favorable as the Michigan Territory. ... The soil of the territory is generally fertile, and a considerable proportion of it is very rich."

ESTWICK EVANS. *A Predestrious Tour of Four Thousand Miles Through the Western States and Territories, During the Winter and Spring of 1818.*

"Never again will the vast succession of coming people know how beautiful this land was in nature. No pen picture can describe the park-like plains and rolling openings or the solemn grandeur of the timber land."

L. D. WATKINS, a settler of the 1820s in southern Michigan.

"If any person, or persons, shall exhibit any puppet show, wire dancing, or tumbling, juggling or sleight of hand, within this territory, and shall ask or receive any pay in money, or other property, for exhibiting the same, such a person, or persons, shall for every offense pay a fine of not less than ten nor exceeding twenty dollars."

Michigan Territorial law, enacted on April 13, 1827.

"The chaps from the Wolverine state are the all-greediest, ugliest, an sourest characters on all Uncle Sam's twenty-six farms, they are, in thar natur, like their wolfish namesakes, always so etarnal hungry that they bite at the air, and hang their underlips, and show the harrow teeth of their mouths, as if they'd jump right into you, an swallor you hull, without salt."

From a folksy almanac of the 1830s.

"Ye who led a single life
And now wish to get a wife,
I tell you this, now understand,
We have first-rate girls in Michigan."

Song from the 1830s promoting Michigan as a place to settle.

"I have left England and its gloomy climes for one of brilliant sunshine and inspiring purity, ... a country where all is life and animation, where I hear on every side the sound of exultaion, where everyone speaks of the past with triumph, the present with delight, the future with growing confidence and anticipation. ... asked how long I mean to remain here I answer as long as I live."

JOHN FISHER, an immigrant to Michigan in the 1830s.

"The peninsula of Michigan, lying between the lake of the same name on the west, and Huron on the east, is one of the greatest beauties of the kind in America, if not the world."

C. COLTON. *Tour of the American Lakes.* 1833.

"If you would seek a beautiful peninsula, look around you."

Inscription on the Great Seal of Michigan, designed by LEWIS CASS in 1835 and presented to the first state constitutional convention.

"... a howling wilderness."

A. L. DRIGGS, a new settler in the territory. 1835.

"The great inland lakes are for this territory what the Mediterranean is for the Old World. An immense industry will develop along these inland lakes, and the Michigan peninsula will be the mediator of trade and commerce between the eastern and western lake regions."

German traveler KARL NEIDHARD's observations on a trip through the Michigan Territory in 1835.

(The soil is) four feet deep, and so fat that it will grease your fingers.

An early farmer describing Michigan's soil. 1836.

"A plane, a chisel and two dollars a day are the requirements of a carpenter in Michigan."

CAROLINE KIRKLAND. *A New Home, Who'll Follow.* 1839

"Our streams are the clearest that
    nature supplies,
And Italy's beauties are marked in our
    skies;
Our woodlands are filled with rare
    plants and sweet flow'rs
Of exquisite beauty and exquisite pow
    ers;
And the isle-spotted lakes that encircle
    our plains
Are the largest and purest this planet
    contains;
And talk, as ye may talk, of countries of
    wealth,
This land is the country of vigor and
    wealth."

From the poem, "The Land of the Lakes." 1840s.

"... I was as much disappointed in Michigan as any country I ever saw. As to its health, but very few make any pretense to its being any other than sickly. The water and the visage of the inhabitants were very indicative of an extremely unhealthy climate. In many sections death has made awful ravages. Some small villages ere almost forsaken by the inhabitants. A small village, near Coldwater, is almost depopulated by the unflinching hand of death."

JAMES LEANDER SCOTT. *A Journal of a Missionary Tour.* 1843.

"I expect nothing from Michigan, and heartily wish I had never heard of the state."

JAMES FENIMORE COOPER, in a letter to his wife. 1848. The reference is probably to an investment in Kalamazoo real estate that didn't turn a profit.

"Thank God for Michigan."

PRESIDENT LINCOLN's response to the arrival of the First Michigan in Washington D.C. It was the first regiment from the West to arrive in Washington after Lincoln's call for volunteers. 1861.

"Now to describe this Michigan
Is beyond the art of man,
But I'll try my endeavor
And do the best I can.
The land is poor I'm very sure;
The people are mean, you know,
And we cursed the day that ever we
    came
To Michigan - I - O."

Song Michigan - I - O. 1870s.

" 'If you seek a beautiful peninsula, here's a couple of them; take your pick.' This might be rendered into resounding Latin if thought best. ..."

E. LAKIN BROWN suggesting an amendment to the state motto at the annual meeting of the Pioneer Society of Michigan in 1877.

"My eastern friends who wish to find
A country that will suit your mind,
Where comforts all are near at hand,
Had better come to Michigan."

Detroit Post and Tribune. February 13, 1881.

"I love the old State from a thousand human viewpoints. ..."

CARL SANDBURG. The famous poet moved to Berrien County in the 1920s.

"It is hardly to be wondered at that one sometimes hears talk of Michigan's dissolving itself into two commonwealths, when nature has omitted nothing that works for mutual compatibility and man has done little to force enduring bonds of unity."

LEW ALLEN CHASE. *Rural Michigan.* 1922.

"Michigan offers manufacturers an atmosphere that expects progress and success and knows not failure."

MATTHEW CAREY, National Association of Real Estate Boards. 1926.

"We could not enforce the prohibition law in Michigan if we had the United States standing army."

ROY VANDERCOCK, Commander of the Michigan State Police. 1930.

"Non-Michiganians, if they give the Peninsula State a thought at all, picture it as little more than a snowy waste sprinkled with pines, sand dunes, Indian wigwams, small inland lakes and automobile factories all lying somewhere in the wilderness north of Toledo and South Bend."

EDNA FERBER. *Come and Get It.* 1935.

"Isn't that uneasy peninsula between the lakes the place where all the trouble that afflicts this nation start?"

A *New York Times* editorial entitled "Oh Michigan" that railed against sit-down strikes. 1937.

"Michigan could salt the whole world."

ANDREW H. BROWN. *National Geographic.* March 1952. From 1905 to 1958 Michigan ranked either first or second among the states in salt production.

"... child of the Great Lakes."

Michigan Historical Commission. *This Is Michigan.* 1953.

"My state is half reality and half the dim, enchanted memories of a long lost boyhood."

BRUCE CATTON. *Holiday Magazine.* August 1957.

"Michigan is perhaps the least typical of all the original forty-eight states of the union."

WILLIS F. DUNBAR and GEORGE S. MAY. *Michigan: A History of the Wolverine State.* 1970.

"By the year 2000, it is probable that the only wild terrain left in the region will be in government parks, and even that may be a sort of ersatz wilderness with public toilets."

JAMES BARRY. *The Fate of the Great Lakes.* 1972

"Life in Michigan north of the industrial zone is easy and pleasant, with fish to be caught and clear lakes for swimming, lonely streams for canoes and the big lake itself for larger craft; here it is possible to escape from steamy, overcrowded, overactive middle west and get back to something we knew long ago, when it was good enough just to breathe the clean air and feel sunlight and wind on your shoulders."

BRUCE CATTON. *Waiting for the Morning Train.* 1972.

"Michigan has never really had a present moment. It has a mysterious past and an incalculable future, attractive and terrifying by turns, but the moment where the two meet is always a time of transition."

BRUCE CATTON. *Michigan: A Bicentennial History.* 1976.

"This is the land where every small town seems to have a college."

Rand McNally. *Guide to Michigan.* 1979.

"When you consider the history of this state, it appears that Michigan ... has occasionally backed into the future, and into success."

NOEL GROVE. *National Geographic.* June 1979.

"... people live for their cars and their weekends."

NOEL GROVE. *National Geographic.* June 1979.

"... the whole state is an economic garage sale with everyone buying each others used mitre boxes, chain saws, and hunting boots, Robert Hall sportcoats, plastic dinnerware and legless dolls."

JIM HARRISON. *Just Before Dark.* 1980.

"The State of Michigan is the keystone of the Great Lakes."

NEAL PEIRCE and JOHN KEEFE. *The Great Lake States of America.* 1980.

"We sought a pleasant peninsula and, looking around us, found it in need of repairs."

JOE ARMSTRONG and JOHN PAHL. *River & Lake: A Sesquicentennial History of Allegan County, Michigan.* 1985.

"... the 40 million people living in the Great Lakes region are exposed to more toxic chemicals than those in any comparable segment of North America."

CHARLES E. WEBB. *National Geographic.* July 1987.

"Michigan is a land where water has been the unifying force of destiny and will most certainly remain so far in the future."

GOVERNOR WILLIAM G. MILLIKEN's introduction to *Michigan: Photography* by Balthazar Korab. 1987.

"Water, the first element of life, shapes us all; in Michigan it is so ever-present that Michiganians forget its significance.

Michiganians seem to have an almost mystical feeling about water and the north woods — that dark, mysterious, wonderful land that lies north of Clare."

MARTHA BIGELOW. "Michigan: A State in the Vanguard," in *Heartland* by James Madison. 1988.

"If the national economy catches cold, Michigan gets pneumonia."

A contemporary saying that's been repeated so often it has become a cliche.

Ever and again when I return to Michigan, the first and overwhelming fact that strikes me, intimating a presence more than visual, is the persistent flatness of the land.

RONALD JAGER. *Eighty Acres.* 1990.

... a place where the past, present and future are all tied up in a hard knot.

BRUCE CATTON. *Michigan History Magazine.* July/August 1992.

Despite the facts that Michigan State College had the first-level academic courses in Agriculture in the United States and that the nation's best strawberries are grown south of Houghton in the Upper Peninsula; despite the highly visible orchards and vineyards in southwest Michigan; despite Traverse City's area's famed cherries; and despite the farm fields everywhere else, Michigan is not ordinarily thought of as an agricultural state.

CLARENCE ANDREWS. *Michigan in Literature.* 1992.

Military Forts

Fort Brady (Sault Ste. Marie)

"The American fortress, called Fort Brady, is to the east of the town, on the water's edge. It is merely a collection of barracks, offices, quarters, and store houses, surrounded by a high white-washed stockade, looking as if the tall branchless stems of some burnt forest has fallen into ranks, and been whitened over as a reward for their good conduct."

WILLIAM H.G. KINGSTON, on a tour of the Great Lakes in 1853.

Fort Michilimackinac

TOM POWERS

"Before the villages and the cities of the Lower Lakes were, Michilimackinac was — yes, more than one hundred and fifty years before the populous cities of Utica, Rochester, Buffalo and Cleveland had a geographic name — more than a century before they were known — even as 'God-forsaken places, inhabited by muskrats and visited only by straggling trappers,'

Michilimackinac and her dependencies had their forts and chapels and college, and their priests, merchants and scientific explorers."

JAMES JESSE STRANG, describing the area around the fort as it was during the 1600s. *Ancient and Modern Michilimackinac.* 1854.

"... this village is one of the largest in all Canada."

CADILLAC, founder of Detroit. 1694.

"When Detroit was a lifeless waterway and Chicago was only a name for wild garlic, Michilimackinac was a center of dominion and power."

A description of the area around the fort during the 1700s by WALTER HAVINGHURST. *Three Flags at the Straits.* 1966.

"It is always healthy at Michilimakinac; this may be attributed to the good air or to the good food; but it is better to attribute it to both. A certain proof of the excellence of the climate is to see the old men there, whose grandsons are growing grey; and it would seem as if death had no power to carry off these spectors. They have good hearing and good sight, but their memory often plays them tricks, for they sometimes claim that they are 150 or 200 years old. They tell tales and recount events which they maintain happened at the time, which is not credible, but they have this advantage, that there is no one who can contradict them or call them liars except by inference."

CADILLAC, founder of Detroit. 1716.

"This place has been since Major Rogers command a receptacle for bankrupts and vagabonds, many of which has got in debt here as much as they could and then gone off to the Indians."

BEAMSLEY GLAZIER, resident of Michilimackinac. 1768.

Fort Wilkins (Copper Harbor)

"Fort Wilkins was built early in 1844 to protect prospectors from the Indians, although in practice the protection worked the other way around."

ANGUS MURDOCK. *Boom Copper.* 1943.

"If placed in charge of those who would preserve and care for it, old Fort Wilkins would become a gathering point for thousands who love historic associations and the call of the wild, here to be had in a single setting."

LEW ALLEN CHASE, Head of the Department of History, Northern State Normal School, Marquette. 1920.

Fort Mackinac

TOM POWERS

"Solemn sentinels pace the ancient walls, and rusty cannon frown sullenly from the battlements, but in spite of mounted guard and severe military etiquette we fear it must be acknowledged that one gunboat could easily level Fort Mackinac to its limestone foundations."

CONSTANCE FENIMORE WOOLSON, author and niece of James Fenimore Cooper. 1870.

Mining

"One often finds at the bottom of the water pieces of pure copper, of ten and twenty pounds weight. I have several times seen such pieces in the savages' hands; and, since they are superstitious, they keep them as so many divinities. ... Some have kept them for more than fifty years; others have had them in their families from time immemorial, and cherish them as household gods."

FATHER ALLOUEZ, making the first report to Europe of copper in the Lake Superior area. 1665.

"The best forests of Michigan are underground."

A common saying among copper and iron miners during the 1800s that noted the vast amount of timber used to shore up mines.

"Late in the afternoon of September 19, 1844, the region just south of Lake Superior ceased to be a howling wilderness. At that hour the needle of a magnetic compass held by William Burt dipped and jittered furiously. Then it quivered with uncertainty a moment and, like a man lost in the woods and gone wholly mad, it darted west and east and south, describing wild arcs, pointing nowhere for long."

STEWART HOLBROOK. *Iron Brew.* 1939. A description of the discovery of iron in the U.P.

"Boys, look around and see what you can see."

United States Deputy Surveyor, WILLIAM BURT's directions to his men when his compass began acting strangely. 1844.

"The masses of virgin copper found in beds of gravel are, however, the most remarkable feature of these mines. ... one of the masses, weighing seventeen hundred and fifty pounds, with the appearance of having once been fluid with heat. It was so pure that it might have been cut in pieces by cold steel and stamped at once into coin."

WILLIAM CULLEN BRYANT. 1846.

"Today the Cliff Mine has no rival in this region nor in the world."

HORACE GREELEY. *New York Tribune.* 1847. The Cliff Mine on the Keweenaw Peninsula was the first commercially successful copper mine in America.

"The more we see and learn of the mineral capacity of the Upper Lake Country, the more amazed we are at its riches and beauty."

Pittsburgh Gazette. 1847.

"We have an abundance of good ores in Pennsylvania and we have no need of your Michigan ores. Besides, you will not see a ton of it in this market in your or my day."

DR. PETER SHOENBERGER, the owner of blast furnaces in Pittsburgh to William Burt. Burt replied, "Mr. Shoenberger, you will have it here in five years at the farthest and beg for it." 1850.

"I believe, all the men, women and children residing in the copper cities, have been crystalized into finished geologists. It matters not how limited their knowledge of the English language may be, for they look only to the surface of things; it matters not how empty of common sense their brain-chambers may be, they are wholly absorbed in sheeting their minds and hearts with bright red copper. ... You stand upon a commanding hill-top, and whilst lost in the enjoyment of a fine landscape, a Copper Harbor 'bear' or 'bull,' recently from Wall Street, will slap you on the shoulder, and startle the surrounding air with the following yell: 'That whole region, sir, is conglomerate, and exceeding rich in copper and silver.' You ask your landlady for a drop of milk to flavor your coffee, and she will tell you 'that her husband has exchanged the old red cow for a conglomerate location somewhere in the interior.' ... You happen to see a little girl arranging some rocky specimens in her baby-house, and your asking her name, she will probably answer — 'Conglomerate the man, my name, sir, is Jane.'"

CHARLES LANMAN. *Adventures in the Wilds of the United States.* 1856.

"If (an iron) mine, by some means or other, did not kill one man a week ... it was considered strange indeed."

STEWART HOLBROOK, describing the industry as it was during the 1860s-1870s. Iron Brew. 1939.

"In 1889 Michigan was not only the greatest copper producing state in the United States, but it mined more copper than any foreign country."

M. M. QUAIFE. *Michigan: From Primitive Wilderness to Industrial Commonwealth.* 1948.

"Indisputable mineralogical fact is that, until about ten years ago, the Michigan Copper Country was the only place on the face of the earth where copper had been found in its pure, workable, native state."

ANGUS MURDOCK. *Copper Boom.* 1943.

"Death is always close at Ishpeming. ... When a mine kills men, it is almost as though their best friend had destroyed them."

JOHN MARTIN. *Call It North Country.* 1944.

"Iron is the giant of Upper Michigan. Somehow it symbolizes the timeless richness of this land — the hope of the future, the struggle and romance of the past."

JOHN MARTIN. *Call It North Country.* 1944.

"It has been said of the Cornish miners that they possess 'the mathematics of the mole.' Whatever that may be the Cornishman seems to have an unusual sense of direction underground and also an unexplainable judgement as to where to look for the ore."

JAMES FISHER. *Michigan History Magazine.* 1945.

"There was a saying that a five-year Finnish mining veteran was so tough that to kill him you had to cut off his head and hide it from him."

WILLIAM ELLIS. *Land of the Inland Seas.* 1974

See also *Cities* (Calumet and Marquette) and *Landmarks* (Keweenaw Peninsula)

Native Americans

"Englishmen, although you have conquered France, you have not conquered the Indians. We are not your slaves. Those lakes, those woods and mountains were left us by our ancestors. We will part with them to none."

Chippewa CHIEF MINAVAVANA at Fort Michilimackinac in 1761.

"Father, we care not for the land, or the money, or the goods; what we want is whiskey."

Potawatomi CHIEF TOPENEBEE to Michigan Indian Agent Lewis Cass in 1821.

"The American Indian of the Great Lakes region survived only two centuries of contact with the white man; then he was swept aside and his way of life forgotten."

RUSSELL McKEE. *Great Lakes Country.* 1966.

"The American settlers dispossessed the tribesman as completely here as anywhere, but they did not slaughter him while they were doing it. They did not have to; they were not afraid of him, and if the red man was there to be trodden on he did not have to be kicked first."

BRUCE CATTON. *Waiting for the Morning Train.* 1972.

Natural Attractions

Good Harbor Bay

"The bay is about five miles wide and the equal of any tourist-photo bay I know of, though ungraced by Noel Coward and suchlike who go to Montego."

JIM HARRISON. *Just Before Dark*. 1972.

Grand Sable Dunes

"For an extent of many miles nothing is visible but a waste of sand, not under the form of a monotonous desert plain, but rising into lofty cones, swept into graceful curves, hurled into eddying hollows and spread into long extended valleys."

BELA HUBBARD. *Lake Superior Journal: Bela Hubbard's Account of the 1840 Houghton Expedition*.

"As one intently regards this extensive barrier of sand, he seems gazing on the confines of some boundless desert — the Syrian or Sahara."

ROBERT E. CLARKE. *Harpers Monthly Magazine*. March 1853.

"... though it seems not to have been classed among the wonders of this region, nor described in any books of travel, so far as I am aware, may well be called extraordinary, and worthy of place among the scenic wonders of America. It is a miniature Sahara, several miles in extent, and in many of its peculiar features resembling those lifeless, sandy deserts which are so distinguishing a phenomena in some parts of the world. It is known to French voyageurs as 'Le Grand Sable.'"

BELA HUBBARD. *Memoirs of Half a Century*. 1887.

Grand Traverse Bay

"A geography as unique as a fingerprint."

Copy from Traverse City's award-winning application as an All-American City. 1984.

Huron Mountains

"The spirit of the north woods envelops the Huron Mountains."

U.S. Dept. of the Interior. *The Fourth Shore*. 1959.

"... the roughest and wildest country in Michigan."

LAWRENCE WAKEFIELD. *All Our Yesterdays*. 1977.

Irish Hills

"There is considerable disagreement as to precisely where they begin and end and, in truth, there are no abrupt lines — either on the map or in the landscape — to tell you when you have entered and left. The traveler fades into the region and fades out again."

BOB ROBERTS. *Motor News*. September 1965.

"... working-class Poconos. ..."

DORIS SCHARFENBERG. *Country Roads of Michigan.* 1992.

"To the average visitor, the Irish Hills are 3.2 miles of gently rolling tourist traps, unspoiled by nature."

NEAL RUBIN. *Detroit Free Press Magazine.* October 4, 1992.

Keweenaw Peninsula

See also *Cities* (Calumet, Copper Harbor, Eagle River, and Gay), *Copper Mining, Military Forts* (Fort Wilkins) and *Roads* (Brockway Mountain Drive)

"... the El Dorado of that day."

CHARLES LANMAN. *The Red Book of Michigan.* 1871. The author is referring to the copper rush of 1845.

"... a cold, sterile region with a great bullying, boisterous sea, subject to sudden tempests and tremendous storms. ..."

Buffalo (New York) *Morning Express.* 1846.

"Gorgeous and glorious the sight! causing us to pause again and again in a rapture of admiration."

ROBERT E. CLARKE, reporting on a hike across the peninsula for the March 1853 edition of *Harpers Monthly.*

"America's Lapland."

Finnish miners' name for the cold, snowy peninsula. 1860s.

"The country is not thoroughly subdued, and has a kind of defiant air, as if it considered itself, on the whole, superior to any civilization which had yet invaded it."

G. M. STEELE. *The Ladies Respository.* August 1871.

"The Treasure Chest of Michigan."

Michigan: A Guide to the Wolverine State. 1941.

"... a mere thumb of land poked like a testing finger into the cold, blue waters of Lake Superior. ... it is as scenically — and historically — exciting as any spot in the United States. ..."

ANGUS MURDOCK. *Boom Copper.* 1943.

"When speaking of the climate up here people used to say that they had eight months of winter and four months of cold weather."

RAY DRIER. *Copper Country Tales, Vol I.* 1967.

"The Keweenaw Peninsula is still untamed and still resists transformation. ... the stubborn intransigence of the Keweenaw to yield itself to short-range human interests offers a lesson: In this case, the land is best met on its own terms."

ELA JOHNSON. *The Faces of the Great Lakes.* 1977.

"There are few places in the contiguous United States more remote and less hospitable or, to the lover of wild places, more starkly and supremely beautiful."

WILLIAM ASHWORTH. *The Late Great Lakes.* 1987.

TOM POWERS

Keweenaw Peninsula Coastline

"The land of lavish snow."

KATHRYN WALTERS. *Country Journal*. February 1989.
The Keweenaw Peninsula averages 20 feet of snow a
winter.

"... the Keweenaw district and its abundance of native copper was and is unique on this earth."

DAVID J. KRAUSE. *The Making of a Mining District:
Keweenaw Native Copper 1500-1870*. 1992.

"Christmas trees, Christmas trees ... nothing but goldarned Christmas trees."

A Texan's reaction on looking out over the Keweenaw
Peninsula from the top of Brockway Mountain Drive.
Date unknown.

Kingston Plains

"Time stopped here. The land died. The stumps are its tombstones, rolling out of sight across the hills. The place is a mental disturbance, one of those pictures that will not go away."

RUSSELL McKEE. *Audubon Magazine*. March 1988.
The Kingston Plains, just south of the Pictured Rocks,
was clear cut in the 1890s and never recovered.

Little Traverse Bay

"The sunsets on the bay are enough to throw an artist's soul into ecstasy."

The Traverse Region, Historical and Descriptive.
1884.

Old Mission Peninsula

"... a special place of wonderful serenity. ..."

From GOVERNOR WILLIAM MILLIKEN'S introduction
to *Michigan* by Batthazar Korab. 1987.

Pictured Rocks

"Along the shore there are many caves caused by the violence of the water. ... When the lake is agitated the waves go into these cavities with great force and make the most horrible noises, like the shooting of great guns.

At one point we came to a remarkable place. It is a bank of rocks that the wild men in our party made a sacrifice to; they call it Naniloucksingoit, which signifies 'likeness of the Devil.' They sling much tobacco and other things on it in veneration. ..."

PIERRE RADISSON. 1658.

"... Pictured rocks ... present some of the most sublime and commanding views in nature. This stupendous wall of rock, exposed to the fury of the waves, which are driven up by every north wind across the whole width of Lake Superior, has been partially prostrated at several points, and worn out into numerous bays, and irregular indentations. All these front upon the lake, in a line of aspiring promontories, which, at a distance, present the terrible array of dilapidated battlements and desolate towns."

HENRY SCHOOLCRAFT. 1820.

"The effect produced on the mind as we approached these rocks can not be described — picturesque in the distance they become sublime, awfully sublime, as we drew near. Our feelings scarcely could find utterance in words when we found ourselves at the foot, and when we attempted to raise our eyes to the dizzy height which frowned directly over our heads. We also shrunk from the view as with a vivid consciousness of human insignificance. ... On the whole I cannot think any scenery I ever visited, even including Niagara Falls and its vicinity, is to be compared for grandeur

TOM POWERS

Miners Castle (Pictured Rocks)

and sublimity to the Pictured Rocks of Lake Superior."

DAVID DOUGLAS BATES. *The Journal of David Douglas Bates.* 1820.

"Nothing I had ever heard at all prepared my mind for the sublimity and beauties of this scene: — the rock, so lofty and precipitous; the wide openings that yawned below, leading we knew not where; but above all the brilliant colours that diversify every foot of this vast range of rocks. ... it far surpassed in brilliancy and beauty any-

thing we had imagined."

DR. CHANDLER ROBBINS GILMAN. *Life on the Lakes: Being Tales and Sketches Collected During a Trip to the Pictured Rocks.* 1836.

"Sped away in gust and whirlwind
On the shores of Gitche-Gumee,
Westward by the Big-Sea-Water
Came unto the rocky headlands,
To the Pictured Rocks of sandstone,
Looking over land and landscape."

HENRY WADSWORTH LONGFELLOW. *Song of Hiawatha.* 1855.

"They have been often described, but no description that I have seen conveys to my mind a satisfying impression of their bold, wild, and curious features. ..."

BELA HUBBARD. *Memoirs of Half a Century.* 1887.

"Pictured Rocks — triumph of a fluid medium over resistant rock."

U.S. Dept. of the Interior. *Our Fourth Shore.* 1959.

"Only a blind man could fail to enjoy the Pictured Rocks — the most blaze world traveler owns their beauty."

BEATRICE H. CASTLE. *The Grand Island Story.* 1974.

Porcupine Mountains

"How shall I paint the Sunset scene on Lake Superior as vivid from the top of the Porcupine Mountains. I have been tossed on Eries billows, I have heard the thunder of Lake Michigan as she in her majesty lashed her impenetrable barrier but never have I seen nature in all her gorgeous beauty until I viewed her at evening from these mountains. As the sun approached the christal floor of Lake Superior the blue waters were painted and tinged with every possible hue and sparkled like diamonds. Shortly the brillients appeared to concentrate until there was but one bright path from us to the Sun and formed a beautiful bridg from Earth to heaven. I had always been accustomed to seeing the Sun abov me but now it was below near the water, on the water, and under the water, And now the Sun sleeps in Lake Superior."

ANDREW RUNDEL, from a journal he kept while prospecting for copper in 1846.

"The Porkies have the same kind of lure as the Grand Canyon: What you do there is less important than the simple fact of being there."

EDWARD HOOGTERP. *Flint Journal.* May 10, 1992.

Saginaw Bay

"... a gulf of terror."

An unknown land surveyor. 1800s.

"In Bay City the water in Saginaw Bay was blown out from shore for a distance of a mile or more and we recall hundreds of Bay City and area residents walking on what had been the bottom of the bay to salvage whatever they could find. And the treasures were there! Outboard motors, boats, guns, fishing tackle, ice boats, you name it and the bottom of Saginaw Bay had it! Best of all sights that day were the 'instant fishermen' who fished with shovels, rakes, and pitchforks and carried home bushel baskets and washtubs of fresh fish."

JACK PARKER, recalling a 1940 occurence. *Shipwrecks of Lake Huron.* 1986.

"... probably the meanest, roughest body of water in the Lakes."

ALIDA MALKUS. *Blue-Water Boundary.* 1960.

"... the most unpredictable body of water this side of the Bay of Biscay."

JACK PARKER. *Shipwrecks of Lake Huron.* 1986.

Saginaw Valley

"... the world's beanbasket."

BILL SEMION. *Michigan Living.* August 1992.

St. Clair Flats

• The St. Clair Flats, located at the spot where the St. Clair River empties into Lake St. Clair, is the largest delta in the Great Lakes.

TOM POWERS

"The word 'marsh' does not bring up a beautiful picture to the mind, and yet the reality was as beautiful as anything I have ever seen, — an enchanted land, whose memory haunts me as idea unwritten, a melody unsung, a picture unpainted, haunts the artist, and will not away.

... it's nothing but one great sponge for miles. ...

... an ocean full of land, — a prairie full of water, — a desert full of verdue."

CONSTANCE FENIMORE WOOLSON. *Castles Nowhere: Lake-Country Sketches.* 1875.

"... and still the crowds come and come. Is there no end to them? Has the whole population of Detroit chosen this special day to go to the Flats? No, this is only a fair sampling of every Sunday morning in summer; this is the Sunday crowd.

Michigan's Venice."

Detroit News Tribune. August 18, 1895.

"No finer hunting and fishing grounds are to be found in the world than around here."

JOHN MANSFIELD. *History of the Great Lakes.* 1899.

"Nowhere else can there be found such a summer resort. The houses are built upon piles driven in the silt, and often there is running water all around. ... This 'city in the water' with its liquid streets and roadways, has no gloomy antiquities or crumbling marbles like ancient Venice, but is sweet and fresh with summer homes."

White Star Magazine. Summer 1906.

"... the Venice of America."

Great Lakes Waterway Guide. 1960.

Sleeping Bear Dunes

TOM POWERS

"A woman I know says that to look at the Sleeping Bear late in the day is to feel the same emotion that comes when you listen to Beethoven's Emperior Concerto."

BRUCE CATTON. *Waiting for the Morning Train.* 1972.

"This is one of the most dramatic coastlines in North America, perhaps in the world. Rising almost directly from the surf behind a tiny striplet of beach, the face of Sleeping Bear heaves skyward like the flank of some enormous buff-colored animal, hulking and severe."

WILLIAM ASHWORTH. *The Late Great Lakes.* 1987.

"Tawny, burnished, curvaceous, the Sleeping Bear Dunes lie like some magnificently indolent female spirit on the northeastern shores of Lake Michigan."

KATHLEEN STOCKING. *Letters from the Leelanau.* 1989.

Sand Dunes

"The dunes are to the Midwest what the Grand Canyon is to Arizona and Yosemite is to California. They constitute a signature of time and eternity. Once lost, the loss would be irrevocable."

CARL SANDBURG. Date unknown.

Snail Shell Harbor

TOM POWERS

"... the most beautiful harbor in the Upper Peninsula."

KENNETH S. LOWE. *Motor News.* May 1963.

Stannard Rock (See p. 126)

Straits of Mackinac

See also *Bridges* (Mackinac), *Cities* (Mackinaw City and St. Ignace), *Islands* (Mackinac Island), and *Military Forts* (Fort Mackinac and Fort Michilimackinac)

"Whoever looks upon the map of North America will be struck with the singular conformation of both land and water round the Straits of Mackinac. There is scarcely any thing in American geography more remarkable."

E. D. MANSFIELD, *Methodist Quarterly Review*, 1861.

"The state of Michigan ran car ferries across the Straits of Mackinac to St. Ignace in the upper peninsula. The car ferries were notorious. ... They left Mackinaw City at hour and a half intervals. There were long waits. One November a man I knew got at the end of the ferry line in Cheboygan, twenty miles away, and it took him thirty-six hours to reach the ferry."

EDMUND G. LOVE, describing the area as it was in 1934. *A Small Bequest.* 1973.

"Summer and winter a fleet of state-run ferryboats honk and churn their way back and forth between Mackinaw City, at the top of the lower peninsula, and St. Ignace, across the straits in the upper peninsula. During the height of the tourist season even the faithless can walk across the straits on the orange peels."

JOHN VOELKER. *Trouble-shooter.* 1943.

"Nature, in the glacial period, tore Michigan apart, bulldozed a deep canyon between the shuddering and constantly retreating segments, and then, thawing her massive plow of solid ice, she filled the gap with flowing water — the Straits of Mackinac, crossroads of the Great Lakes."

EUGENE GAY-TIFFT. *Partners, the Magazine of Labor & Management.* November 1957.

Stannard Rock

• Stannard Rock is a huge submerged "mountain" whose "peak" lies just below the surface of Lake Superior 30 miles from the nearest land. A lighthouse was constructed there in 1882, and lightkeepers were assigned to live at the structure until the beacon was automated in 1958.

"The loneliest place in America."

Motor News. August 1959

"... the most isolated lighthouse in the world."

C. FRED RYDHOLM. *The Superior Heartland.* 1989.

PENROSE

Straits of Mackinac (cont.)

"... the man who invented the safety razor was supposed to have done so after trying to shave with a straight one while passing through the Straits on a moderately calm day."

WILLIAM RATIGAN. *Straits of Mackinac.* 1957.

"There's no such thing as a calm day at the Straits of Mackinac. The wind up there invented perpetual motion."

WILLIAM RATIGAN. *Highways Over Broad Waters.* 1959.

"It is a spacious scene: vast sky, wider water, a shoreline dark with forest."

WALTER HAVINGHURST. *Three Flags at the Straits.* 1966.

"Perhaps one of the most historic spots in all America, the Straits of Michilimackinac is the richest historical treasure house of the Great Lakes."

JACK PARKER. *Shipwrecks of Lake Huron.* 1986.

Tawas Point

"Cape Cod of Michigan."

Great Lakes Waterway Guide. 1960.

"... one of the most splendid sandspits in the world."

WILLIAM ASHWORTH. *Late Great Lakes.* 1987.

Thumb

"Whoever called Americans a 'rootless' people never saw the west shore of the Thumb, where houses used eight weeks a year block off the lake every day of the year."

WILLIAM LEAST HEAT MOON. *Blue Highways.* 1982.

"The geographic bulge that makes Michigan's map look like a mitten is full of uncluttered visions, scenes before shopping malls and fast tracks. Night life is a friendly card game and going to a movie takes too much driving to bother with."

DORIS SCHARFENBERG. *Michigan Living.* August 1988.

"Four-lane highways don't make it into the Thumb, stop signals are curiosities and only grain silos have elevators."

DORIS SCHARFENBERG. *Country Roads of Michigan.* 1992.

Thunder Bay

"Nearly half way between Saganuam Bay and the northwest corner of the lake, lies another which is termed Thunder Bay. The Indians ... and every European traveller that has passed through it, have unanimously agreed to call it by this name, on account of the continual thunder they have always observed here."

JONATHON CARVER, an early traveler on the Great Lakes. 1778.

"Over 100 major wrecks, sinkings, strandings, burnings, collisons, plus an incomplete tally of human casualties, make this one of the tougher, touchier freshwater cruising areas of the lakes.
Lake Huron's wreck alley."

JACK PARKER. *Shipwrecks of Lake Huron.* 1986.

Whitefish Point

"... graveyard of the Great Lakes."

ARMAND GEBERT. *Michigan Living.* June 1991.

Origin of Name

"The name of Michigan is derived from the Indian word *Michsawgyegan* the meaning of which is the Lake Country."

CHARLES LANMAN. *The Red Book of Michigan.* 1871.

"Michigan owes its name to the Indians. The name is taken from two Chippewa words, *mitchaw* meaning 'great,' and *sagiegan*, meaning 'lake,' hence Land of the Great Lakes."

WILLIAM ETTEN. *A Citizens History of Grand Rapids.* 1926.

"... the name Michigan is taken from the Chippewa word *Michi-gummee*, meaning 'great lake.' "

Rand McNally. *Guide to Michigan.* 1979.

Railroads

"A clever fellow was acquainted with the expansive force of steam; he also saw the wealth of wheat and grass rotting in Michigan. Then he cunningly screws on the steam-pipe to the wheat crop. Puff now, O steam! The steam puffs and expands as before, but this time it is dragging all Michigan at its back to hungry New York and hungry New England."

RALPH WALDO EMERSON. *Wealth*. 1860.

"Anyone desiring to know which way the train was moving was obliged to get off and make a chalk mark upon the track."

JOHN LONGYEAR, Ingham County resident, on the slowness of the Amboy, Lansing, and Traverse Bay Railroad Line, which reached Lansing in 1863. The Line was also called the "Almighty Long and Tremendous Bad" by local residents.

"In those days (1870s) it was a serious thing to a passenger on a train north of Bay City. It was a common occurrence to stand a man on his head in the car, and shake all he had in his pockets on the floor, or where he refused a drink, to hold his mouth open and pour liquor down his throat."

JOHN W. FITZMAURICE. *The Shanty Boy*. 1889.

"The running of trains for any purpose, especially excursion trains, on any road on the Sabbath day, is one of the greatest moral evils of the day."

Resolution drafted by Tuscola County clergymen in the 1880s.

Rivers

Au Sable River

"If you must make comparisons, then I will say that the only rivers on Earth comparable to the Au Sable are the fabled chalk streams of England."

VINCE MARINARO. Date unknown.

"It is a foregone conclusion that no other stream in the state has afforded such delightful pastime and fascinating sport for the devotees of rod and gun as the Au Sable and its tributaries."

HAZEN MILLER. *The Old Au Sable.* 1963.

"Those who know the river will tell you the Au Sable will survive anything. ... It never complains, never talks of its past, never worries about its future. It demands nothing, yet gives its fullest to those who would but take it. And all the while flows silently to the east, slowed, but not stopped, by power dams, alternating allowing its sands to cover and uncover its past, not caring that those who drift on the surface are passing over what can only be called Michigan's Greatest History."

The First Hundred Years: An Introduction to the History of the Grayling Area. 1972.

"Saginaw River."

The Smithsonian Guide to Historic America: The Great Lakes. 1989. On a map of northern Michigan, the Au Sable is mislabeled as the Saginaw River.

"If God had set out to create a river for fly fishermen, this would be it."

CALVIN GATES JR., owner of Gates Au Sable Lodge. 1991.

Detroit River

"The river ... yields to none in point of utility and beauty."

ESTIVICK EVANS. *A Predestrious Tour of Four Thousand Miles, Through the Western States and Territories, During the Winter and Spring of 1818.*

"It is hardly possible for any thing to exceed in beauty the river Detroit, and its shores, and islands."

THOMAS McKENNEY. *Sketches of a Tour to the Lakes.* 1826.

"London has its Thames, Paris the Seine, Rome the Tiber, and New York the Hudson; but in everything the Detroit excels them all. ... All early settlers bore testimony to the beauty of the river and the volume of its waters, which the population of a score of the largest cities cannot diminish or defile.

There are but few streams in the world that rival the Detroit in purity. ..."

SILAS FARMER. *History of Detroit, Wayne County, and early Michigan.* 1890.

"When the population along the river above Detroit becomes greatly increased the waters of the Detroit River will become unfit for domestic use."

ROBERT KEDZIE, doctor and chemistry professor. 1898.

"The Lord probably could have built a better river suited for rum running. But the Lord probably never did."

ROY HAUNES, Michigan Prohibition Commissioner. 1920.

"... the 'H 2-0' highway."

LEM BARNES. *Motor News.* May 1963.

"An occasional fish can be seen in this gauntlet holding its nostrils with one fin and fending off what might be called underactivated sludge with the other as it dashes frantically from the pollution of Lake Erie to the relative safety of Lake St. Clair."

JOHN MacISAAC. *Half the Fun Was Getting There.* 1968.

"You can etch copper in the Detroit River."

Folk wit of the 1960s and '70s.

"... the watery main street of Michigan's greatest city. ..."

Rand McNally. *Guide to Michigan.* 1979.

"It looks like a river, and we call it a river, but the narrow channel between Lakes St. Clair and Erie is a straits — a downspout draining the contents of our sweet seas into still another basin."

DORIS SCHARFENBERG. *The Long Blue Edge of Summer.* 1992.

General

"It's official: Michigan's rivers are unmatched for natural splendor east of the rockies."

EMILIA ASKARI. *Detroit Free Press.* February 20, 1992. From an article reporting on a bill passed by Congress designating 1,000 miles of Michigan rivers for conservation under the Wild and Scenic Rivers Act. Only Alaska and Oregon have more miles of rivers protected under the act.

Jordan River

TOM POWERS

"The party who went up the Jordan yesterday, having entirely exhausted their stock of adjectives, offer a ten dollar chromo to any one who will invent a new one which will adequately express their admiration."

A notice posted in an East Jordan hotel in the 1880s. In 1972 the Jordan River was the first river in Michigan designated as a wild and scenic river by the federal government.

Kalamazoo River

"... a beautiful little river that flows westward, emptying its tribute into the vast expanse of Lake Michigan."

JAMES FENIMORE COOPER. *Oak Openings.* 1848.

Manistee River

"Known as one of the most remarkable streams in the Northwest ... (because) it never floods, seldom freezes, and is never afflicted by droughts."

History of Manistee County, Michigan. 1882.

Portage River and Ship Canal

"I have been up the Saguenay, I have been over the Marshall Pass and through the Royal Gorge of the Arkansas, and I have seen many noble scenes in Europe, but no scenery has ever impressed me with such solemnity as the landscape on that canal in the Twilight of an August afternoon. ..."

ALICE WELLINGTON ROLLINS. *Lippincotts Magazine.* 1885.

River Rouge

"... Narrow, winding, and almost stagnant ... It has at all times the appearance and complexion of a pool; and its exhalations, in the summer months, are extremely unhealthful. ..."

CHARLES JOUETT, a Detroit Indian agent in a letter to Congress on June 25, 1803.

"If I ever tried to dip a worm in the (Rouge River) he'd've crawled back up the line and slapped my face."

LOREN ESTLEMAN. *Motown.* 1991. The setting of the novel was the 1960s.

"We can't program the computer to recognize the Rouge River as water. The Rouge is so filthy that if the computer recognizes it as water, it won't recognize anything else in the world."

Computer programmer for the Landsat satellites. 1987.

St. Clair River

"Sooner or later, all ships on the Great Lakes pass through the St. Clair River."

JAMES L. DONAHUE. *Steaming Through Smoke and Fire, 1871.* 1990.

"That slender neck of water converging at Port Huron for the passage of the Straits is the greatest throat of commerce in the world."

JOHN H. GOFF. *History of the Saint Mary's Falls Canal.* 1907.

St. Mary's River

See also *Soo Locks*

"The Fall of the St. Mary's is the only apparent outlet for the redundant waters of Lake Superior, the vast extent of which — being more than twelve hundred miles in circumference, — makes it problematical how it can answer the purpose. ..."

JOHN JOHNSTON. *An Account of Lake Superior.* 1807.

"The falls themselves are as lovely and as gentle, (shall I say?) as the sudden rush of such a tremendous flood, down an equable descent of twenty-two feet in a mile, can well be imagined; and if the Spirit of the Tempest and of the Furies might be supposed to preside over Niagara's thundering Cataract, the imagination of a Catholic might well be allowed to install the Holy Virgin over the rapids, which are honored by her name. ..."

C. COLTON. *Tour of the American Lakes*. 1833.

"The strait of St. Mary's to the falls is the most difficult to navigate. Its common sailing channel is a perfect labyrinth, devious and circuitous, around islands and sunken rocks, passing across channels and shoals. ... none but the most experienced can pilot a vessel either up or down it."

Gazetteer of Michigan. 1838.

"The descent is about 27 feet in three-quarters of a mile, but the rush begins above, and the tumult continues below the fall, so that, on the whole, the eye embraces an expanse of white foam measuring about a mile each way, the effect being exactly that of the ocean breaking on a rocky shore; not so terrific, nor on so large a scale, as the rapids of Niagara, but quite as beautiful — quite as animated. ..."

ANNA JAMESON. *Winter Studies and Summer Rambles*. 1839.

"O' they are beautiful indeed, these rapids! The grace is so much more obvious than the power."

S. M. FULLER. *Summer on the Lakes in 1843*.

"The river Saint Mary ... rushes over a ledge of rocks in great fury, and presents, for the distance of nearly a mile, a perfect sheet of foam. ... The entire height of the fall is about thirty feet, and after the waters have expressed in a murmuring roar their unwillingness to leave the bosom of Superior, they finally hush themselves to

sleep, and glide onward, as if in a dream, along the picturesque shores of a lovely country, until they mingle with the waters of Lake Huron.

To pass down the falls of Saint Mary, with an experienced voyager, is one of the most interesting, yet thrilling and fearful feats that can be performed."

CHARLES LANMAN. *A Summer in the Wilderness: Embracing a Canoe Voyage Up the Mississippi and Around Lake Superior*. 1847.

"The scenery of the St. Mary's River seems to grow more attractive every year. There is a delicious freshness in the countless evergreen islands that dot the river in every direction, from the falls of Lake Huron, and I can imagine of no more tempting retreats from the dusty streets of towns in summer, than these islands. I believe the time will soon come when neat summer cottages will be scattered along the steamboat route on these charming islands."

J. DISTURNELL. *The Great Lakes or Inland Seas of America*. 1868.

Shiawassee River

"Such was the Shiawassee of my boyhood — my river — clean and refreshing as it flowed along on all the pride of its ancient lineage. Would to God the greed and selfishness of modern commerce had refrained from polluting it! Verily, nothing is sacred to the overlords of business."

JAMES OLIVER CURWOOD. *Son of the Forest*. 1930. The Owosso native and novelist was recalling the river of his youth (circa 1880s) in his autobiography.

Sucker River

"This river of this unpoetic cognomen boasted two branches of equally touching names, the Blind Sucker and the Dead Sucker."

IDA RANSOM SPRING. *Michigan History Magazine.* January/March 1946.

"If there is ever a contest for ugly names in a pretty place, a few votes would go for Bland Sucker River, Dead Sucker River, and Blind Sucker Flooding."

DORIS SCHARFENBERG. *Country Roads of Michigan.* 1992.

Yellow Dog River

"The remote Yellow Dog River is a fabulous little rocking-chair stream; as willful and turbulent and wench as a handsome native dancer; the kind of seductive trout stream that keeps fishermen misty-eyed and mumbling to themselves trying to fathom its tempestuous moods and realize its promise."

JOHN VOELKER. *Trout Madness.* 1960.

Roads

General

"Overland travel in Michigan, even by the Indians, was a sort of last resort, involving as it did, in every season except winter, walking or riding over dim trails, struggling through swamps, making perilous fords, and carrying means of subsistence besides means of shelter and protection against beast and human enemy."

CALVIN GOODRICH, describing the state as it was in the 1760s. *The First Michigan Frontier.* 1940.

"One story that went the rounds was that a person found a beaver hat on the Detroit-Pontiac road, and when, at the risk of his life, he waded out to it, he found a man under it and yelled for help. But the man under the hat protested: 'Just leave me alone, stranger, I have a good horse under me, and have just found bottom.'"

A description of Michigan roads in the 1830s by WILLIS F. DUNBAR and GEORGE S. MAY. *Michigan: A History of the Wolverine State.* 1970.

"The roads in Michigan, and most especially the forty miles from Detroit to Ann Arbor are, because of the lack of stone, the most abominable roads I have ever seen in the United States. Every three paces one encounters tremendous holes and big tree stumps and it requires great skill to circumnavigate them. ..."

KARL NEIDHARD, a German traveler recounting his trip through Michigan. 1835.

"For a distance of 20 miles our route led us over the worst road imaginable, what to the emigrant must be a 'slough of Despond.'"

JOHN M. GORDON, a newly arrived Michigan settler describing the road between Detroit and Plymouth. 1836.

"Juggernaut's car would have been 'broke to bits' on such a road."

HARRIET MARTINEAU, reporting on a trip from Detroit to Ypsilanti. 1836.

"I have read of the caravanserais on old Asian roads, where at night the wayfarers gathered, talking in groups of their journeyings, the land they left, and tomorrow's take off. The camel drivers with their blue-bead bedecked beasts huddled in a courtyard corner, crooning among themselves the haunting Arabic songs they sang to encourage the camels on the long trek. ... Here again in this Michigan Territory town is the inn-gathering, the evening intercourse, the long road the next day."

Letter from a New Yorker, reporting on a trip through Michigan in 1837.

"It goes almost without saying that the roads on the route were simply appalling and 'break downs' and consequent delays were frequent. For days, we walked more miles than we rode, my mother carrying me on her hip with one arm while with the other hand, she tested the depth of mud before each step. My father was often obligated to lead his team over 'corduroy' roads where logs floated and rolled in liquid mud. The poor horses, frightened by the unstable footing, plunged and floundered, and at times sank one or more legs between the loose logs, their extrication proving to be a serious problem, if no fence rail or other means of leverage was at hand."

SARAH ANN COCHRANE remembering the trip from Detroit to Vermontville in Eaton County. 1838.

"Since I have casually alluded to a Michigan mud-hole, I may as well enter into a detailed memoir on the subject for the benefit of future travels. ... Here, on approaching one of these characteristic features of the 'West' the driver stops-alights-walks up to the dark gulf and around it if he can get around it. He then seeks a long pole and sounds it, measures it across to ascertain how its width compares with the length of his wagon-trees, whether its sides are perpendicular, as is usually the case if the road is much used. If he finds it not more than three feet deep, he remounts cheerily, encourages his team and in they go, with a plunge and shock rather apt to damp the courage of the inexperienced."

CAROLING KIRKLAND. *A New Home, Who'll Follow?* 1839.

"When winter came and the sleighing was good, father yoked the oxen, hitched them to a rough sled, drove to Marshall, twenty-eight miles distant, purchased a load of wheat ... and was home again in four days."

EDWARD W. BARBER an early settler in Eaton County. 1840s.

"From Eaton Rapids to Lansing it was mainly mud holes. We regarded ourselves as fortunate if we got our trunks through, even by carrying a pole or rail for considerable distances to pry the old stage out of mud holes."

CHARLES JAY MONROE, a student at MSU in the 1850s on a trip to Lansing.

"(The roads) would have been extremely hard to find if some scoundrel had not thrown a plank across them once in a while."

MARK TWAIN'S tongue-in-cheek reply to the question of how he found Michigan's plank roads on a trip to Grand Rapids in the 1870s.

"Our roads are built of corduroy,
And if you travel far
You sweat and swear and curse and
    damn —
That's how you travel in Michigan."

From the song "Don't Come to Michigan," which was popular during the latter half of the 19th century.

"Another dispiriting element was the road, of which a large part was what is known as 'corduroy,' from some obscure resemblance, which does not exist, between its structure and a certain well-known fabric affected by 'horsey' gentlemen. The jolting we got over this was painful to a degree which it is disagreeable to recall. It jarred every bone in one's body, and embittered the whole aspect of life. It alternated with a series of diabolical mud-holes, into which we drive, and racked, and swayed and splashed interminably. Bunyon's Slough of Despond is all very well in its way, but the possibilities of figurative description of that kind are as a closed book to one who has never ridden on a corduroy road in a wagon with inferior springs."

Scribners Monthly. April 1878. The description of a road heading west out of Tawas.

"Wagons creaking, groaning, crashing,
Wrecks bestrewing either bank
Jarring, jolting, jambling, dashing
This is riding on the Plank."

Farmer/poet ASA STODDARD, describing a trip on an old plank road linking Kalamazoo and Grand Rapids. 1880.

"Somewhere north of Kalkaska and south of Boyne Falls, we entered an eight-mile stretch of highway that was unimproved in the total sense. It consisted of two tracks in the sand that wound back and forth to avoid trees and stumps."

HENRY PRATT's memoir of a 1919 auto trip to the U.P. The description is of the Mackinac Trail, one of the three major north/south highways of the time.

"The Highway Department at Lansing, now one of the most important in our State Government, issues a map every month reporting the conditions of the highways of the State."

CLAUDE S. LARZELERE. *The Story of Michigan.* 1925.

"If the nation is now wholly given over to the making and using of highways, here, maybe is where the process began."

BRUCE CATTON. *Michigan: A Bicentennial History.* 1976.

"... in the U.P. ... families often spend weekends exploring the seemingly endless network of old two-tracks. The usual practice is to load up the family car with gas, food, and beverages, pile in with the kids, take off for the woods, and get promptly lost. They drive around all day at five or ten miles per hour, drive on until the two-track intersects a country road and then try to guess where the hell they are. If there's enough daylight left, they turn back into th woods and get lost again."

JERRY DENNIS. *A Place on the Water.* 1993.

Brockway Mountain Drive (See p. 144)

I-75

"Concrete Tunnel."

Owners of businesses bypassed by newly opened I-75 feared the loss of tourist trade derisively referred to the new road as the "concrete tunnel." 1963.

"Most scenic highway in the United States."

The 22.5-mile section of I-75 between Vanderbilt and Indian River was named the most scenic highway in the U.S. by *Parade Magazine* in the October 1963 issue.

"Michigan's Main Street."

DIXIE FRANKLIN. *Michigan Living.* June 1988.

"From Clare on up it was all pines and pasty stands and straight blacktop like a gash in a green carpet. ..."

LOREN ESTLEMAN. *Downriver.* 1988.

Jefferson Avenue (Detroit)

"... a beautiful and pleasant street, and will compare with the most noted streets of any of our western cities."

Michigan Gazetteer. 1838.

"... one of the proudest thoroughfares in all America."

GEORGE W. STARK. *City of Destiny.* 1943.

M-37

• The state highway extends the length of Old Mission Peninsula, the slim finger of land separating East and West Grand Traverse bays.

"... a glorious digression."

Smithsonian Guide to Historic America: The Great Lakes States. 1989.

Brockway Mountain Drive

- Located on the Keweenaw Peninsula, it is the highest above-sea-level road between the Appalachain Mountains and the Rockies.

GARY W. BARFKNECHT

A View from Brockway Mountain Drive

"... a sky-top highway of unforgettable vistas."

Rand McNally. *Guide to Michigan.* 1979.

"Surely the most scenic piece of pavement in the state. ..."

DORIS SCHARFENBERG. *Long Blue Edge of Summer.* 1992.

M-46

- The state highway runs coast to coast across the middle of the Lower Peninsula.

"... M-46 makes no big promises. It barely touches two small lakes, doesn't skim past any state parks, has to endure the traffic of two cities, and is dead broke on lofty vistas and scenic pull-outs."

DORIS SCHARFENBERG. *Country Roads of Michigan.* 1992.

M-119

• This scenic state highway runs along the crest of a bluff overlooking Lake Michigan from Harbor Springs to Cross Village.

"M-119 is a slowpoke's dream."

DORIS SCHARFENBERG. *Country Roads of Michigan.* 1992

"... you won't find a more scenic 20 miles of Michigan highway south of Big Mac. ..."

TOM POWERS. *More Natural Michigan.* 1992.

TOM POWERS

M-119

M-131

• The state highway traverses nearly the entire length of the Lower Peninsula, starting at the Indiana border and ending at Petoskey.

"Prettiest drive in all of Michigan."

MORT NEFF. *Michigan Living.* October 1978.

Red Arrow Highway

• The Red Arrow Highway parallels the Lake Michigan coast in the southwestern corner of the state.

"... a nostalgic stretch of auto-age Americana, where roadhouses, drive-ins, and tourist courts of the 1920s and 1930s miraculously live on."

MARY and DON HUNT. *Hunt's Highlights of Michigan.* 1991.

US-10

"A wilderness of fifteen leagues separates the Flint River from Saginaw, and the road there is only a narrow path, scarcely recognizable to the eye."

ALEXIS DE TOCQUEVILLE. *Journey to America.* 1831.

"The idea of building a plank road through that swampy country is ridiculously absurd — might as well talk of building a plank road to the moon."

Michigan legislative report on the proposal to build what would eventually become US-10. 1848.

US-12

• Evolving from a Sauk Indian trail and known by various names, US-12 was the first major road linking Chicago and Detroit.

"(The Chicago Road) stretches itself by devious and irregular windings east and west like a huge serpent lazily pursuing its onward course utterly unconcerned as to its destination."

An early 19th century description by an unknown traveler.

"The road from this point to Ypsilanti looks at certain times as if it had been the route of a retreating army, so great is the number of wrecks of different kinds which it exhibits."

A Detroit newspaper description. 1836.

US-23

"Perhaps no other highway in Michigan so defines the region it serves. ... Meandering through forest and farmland, past lakes Great and small, the countryside it travels is largely locked in a time warp,

where big-buck megaresorts and ultra-chic restaurants are aberrations."

BILL SEMION. *Michigan Living*. August 1992.

US-25

"Avenue de Booze."

When Michigan went dry in 1918, two years before the rest of the nation, US-25 between Monroe and Toledo became famous as a rum-runners' pipeline to Detroit.

Woodward Avenue (Detroit)

"... the main street of a ghost town."

JOHN WILLIAMS. *Into the Badlands*: Travels Through Urban America. 1991.

See also *Architecture* (Detroit-Windsor Tunnel) and *Bridges*

Ships and Shipping

General

"Wreck was the common fate of the venturesome schooner or steamboat during the first half of the present (19th) century."

JOHN MANSFIELD. *History of the Great Lakes.* 1899.

"In the early days on the Lakes (long before weather forecasts), every departure was a courageous adventure into the unknown."

A description of shipping during the 1800s in *Inland Seas.* Summer 1986.

"... the construction of these vessels is so frail ... that without the most extreme caution the traveller is every hour in danger of losing his canoe, baggage, and perhaps his life."

CHARLES C. TROWBRIDGE, commenting on the birch bark canoes used by an expedition to Lake Superior in 1820.

"The navigation of Lake Michg. is in the present state of things very perilous. The sailors have no skill, the vessels are badly built and when overtaken far out by a blow and those short ugly waves, they make one plunge, and go down to the bottom without a moment's warning."

JOHN M. GORDON. 1836.

"The wildest expectations of one year seem absurdly tame the next."

GENERAL POE, designer of the Poe Locks at Sault Ste. Marie commenting on the rapid expansion of shipping on the lakes in the 1890s.

"Probably no equal area of the ocean contains as many sunken hulks as do the waters washing the shores of Michigan. ..."

CLAUDE S. LARZELERE. *The Story of Michigan.* 1925.

"Nature seemingly designated the lakes for the age of steel, with iron ranges ringing Lake Superior, deep coal beds in the Ohio valley and limestone halfway between the two, on the edge of Lake Huron."

WALTER HAVINGHURST. *Land of Promise.* 1946.

"There are probably no equal areas of commercial waterways that, if drained, would reveal as many lost vessels as would the Great Lakes."

Federal Writers Project. *Michigan: A guide to the Wolverine State.* 1941.

"It is impossible to exaggerate the supreme importance of this thousand-mile-long ship road. It is a geological miracle indeed that it should have been formed right in the heart of the American continent, that at one end there should be these deposits of iron ore, and that in close proximity to the other end there should be the great coal seams."

HARLAN HATCHER. *A Century of Iron and Men.* 1950.

"Professional seamen treated (the upper Great Lakes) with the respect a lion tamer pays an excitable cat."

WILLIAM RATIGAN. *Straits of Mackinac.* 1957.

"Those who sail the Lakes are men of iron — men of iron nerve, iron will, and iron faith."

WILLIAM RATIGAN. *Great Lakes Shipwrecks and Survivals.* 1977.

"The Great Lakes offer more variety of dangers to mariners and their vessels than any ocean. The thousands of men and ships that the Lakes have claimed over the past two centuries are a grim monument to the hazards of traveling on them."

CHARLES HYDE. *The Northern Lights.* 1986.

Edmund Fitzgerald

"The undisputed queen of the freshwater seas, carrying a banker's name on her bow and stern and a king's ransom in ore between — that was the Fitzgerald in her days of youth and glory.
... the biggest object ever dropped into fresh water in recorded history."

WILLIAM RATIGAN, describing the launching onto the Great Lakes of the *Edmund Fitzgerald* in 1958. *Great Lakes Shipwrecks and Survivals.* 1977.

"I am holding my own."

CAPTAIN ERNEST M. McSORLEY's last radio transmission before the *Edmund Fitzgerald* sank with all hands. 1975.

Griffin

• Built in 1679, the *Griffin* was the first sailing ship on the Great Lakes and was lost with all hands on its maiden voyage. Its final resting place has never been discovered.

"The lakes' commerce opened with a disaster, when the *Griffin* sailed past Washington Island and was never seen again. That began a long tradition."

WALTER HAVINGHURST. *Long Ships Passing.* 1943.

"... the most coveted prize in waters that have yielded a thousand wrecks."

WILLIAM ELLIS. *Land of the Inland Seas.* 1974.

Milwaukee

"Ship is taking water fast. We have turned and headed for Milwaukee. Pumps are all working, but sea-gate is bent and won't keep water out. Flickers are flooded. Seas are tremendous. Things look bad. Crew about the same as last pay day."

In October 1929 the car ferry *Milwaukee* disappeared with all hands in Lake Michigan. A week later a battered can washed ashore with the above note inside, signed by the boat's purser.

Walk-in-the-Water

"The swift steamboat *Walk-in-the-Water* is intended to make a voyage, early in the summer, from Buffalo, on Lake Erie, to Michilimackinac on Lake Huron, for the conveyance of company. The trip has so near a resemblance to the famous Argonautic expedition in the heroic ages of Greece, that expectation is quite alive on the subject."

The Gazette. May 14, 1819. *The Walk-in-the-Water* was the first steamship on the Great Lakes.

GARY W. BARFKNECHT

Soo Locks

"A ship canal around the falls of St. Mary of less than a mile in length, though local in its construction, would be national in its purpose and benefits."

PRESIDENT MILLARD FILLMORE. 1851.

"With justice the Americans consider this remarkable Sault Sainte Marie Canal as a great national enterprise. ... For this reason it is so much more to be regretted that it was not more solidly and more pleasingly carried out, ... although I am no competent expert I will risk saying this, ... (they) will appear as a superficial and careless piece of work. ..."

JOHANN GEORG KOHL, a professional traveler and geographer from Germany, on his impressions of the newly open locks. 1855.

"The opening of the Sault canal has been the largest benefit to the whole United States of any single happening in its commmercial or industrial history."

PETER WHITE, in an address at the semi-centennial celebration of the building of the Sault Canal. 1905.

"... the greatest artificial chamber in the world."

JOHN H. GOFF. *History of the Saint Mary's Falls Canal*. 1907. The author was referring to the Poe Lock, which on completion in 1896 was 800 feet long and 100 feet wide. It was enlarged to over 1,000 feet in length in 1968.

"... the greatest gateway of commerce in the world."

STEWART HOLBROOK. *The Iron Brew*. 1939.

"... the jugular vein of America."

EUGENE SUNDSTROM, a marine affairs reporter from Sault Ste. Marie, on the importance of the canal to the war effort. At one time during WWII, several thousand troops protected the locks.

"No portion of the continental United States ... was as strategically vital to the war effort as the area immediately around Sault Ste. Marie."

ALAN CLIVE, characterizing the locks during WWII. *State of War: Michigan in World War II*. 1979.

"The Sault canal system, which links Lake Superior and Lake Huron at the twin towns of Sault Sainte Marie, in Michigan and Ontario, is the most important mile in America."

National Geographic Society. 1950.

"... no single act of man has conferred so wide a blessing, industrially considered, on the American people as the construction of the first canal at Sault Ste Marie."

RALPH D. WILLIAMS. *The Honorable Peter White*. 1986.

See also *Cities* (Sault Ste Marie) and *Rivers* (St. Mary's River)

"On Labor Day, when the crowds come off the bridge, it's like lava down a slope."

BILL SHEPLER, of Shepler's Mackinac Island Ferry, describing the crowds for the Labor Day Bridge Walk. 1989.

Tourism

"Nearly every city and village in Michigan gets an avalanche of new money each summer and a growing amount in winter from tourists."

BERT HUDGINS. *Michigan Geographic Backgrounds in the Development of the Commonwealth.* 1961.

"... northern Michigan may have been a fine place for some people to make money — with luck, even to strike it rich — but was even a better place to relax and enjoy life."

BRUCE CATTON. *Michigan: A Bicentennial History.* 1976.

"On the first day, according to a northern Michigan nightclub entertainer, the Lord created fudge. And on the second day, He created northern Michigan so people could get to the fudge."

KAY SEVERINSEN. *Michigan Living.* August 1979.

"There's an epidemic of this wilderness fever going around. So we end up with these goddamn kids with beards and backpacks who bring (to the U.P.) one set of underwear and a five dollar bill and don't change either one."

STATE SENATOR JOE MACK, from the U.P. 1981.

GARY W. BARFKNECHT

Bronner's

"What Disney is to amusement parks, Bronner's is to our number-one holiday."

GARY BARFKNECHT, describing Bronner's in Frankenmuth, the largest year-round Christmas store in America. *Ultimate Michigan Adventures.* 1989.

"For three months of the year northern Michigan is a vast summer suburb of Detroit, Chicago, Indianapolis. ..."

JIM HARRISON. *Just Before Dark.* 1991.

See also *Architecture* (Bronners and Grand Hotel), *Islands* (Mackinac Island) and *Natural Attractions* (Irish Hills)

Universities

(Michigan State University and University of Michigan)

Michigan State University

"The College, when I first saw it May 10, 1857, consisted of a tract of mainly timbered land, without an acre fully cleared."

CHARLES JAY MONROE, a member of the first class to enroll at the then-named Michigan Agricultural College. 1857.

"Of the 676 acres belonging to the college, only about one-half an acre was cleared at the time of the dedication in 1857. The two buildings, college hall, and Boarding hall, and the brick barn, had the appearance of being built in the midst of the woods, with nothing on the immediate premises but some burned trees, rubbish from building, and mud holes and huckleberry bushes."

JAMES H. GUNNISON, recalling the dedication of the college. 1857.

University of Michigan

"It was ... reserved to Michigan ... to rear up within 38 years from its inception and the location of its site, an institution rivaling Yale and Harvard, but outstripping them both."

JOHN D. PIERCE, Michigan's first Superintendent of Public Instruction. 1877.

"Before I came down here I used to think that the Buick Motor Car Co. was bound up in a lot of red tape when it came to getting into the place, but Buick has to take a back seat after registering in the University of Michigan. The worst of it is that I've just started and I think by the time I'm finished I'll be cutting paper dolls or something."

From a letter by EMERSON F. POWRIE. 1934.

"The corporate entity which uses the title 'University of Michigan' is a sham. Those who run it — and so many of those who work in it — are no longer interested in teaching, and they care not the least about students."

PROFESSOR BERT HORNBACK, on resigning from the U of M. *Detroit Free Press*. January 19, 1992.

"Even if a kryptonite meteor landed on its main campus, the University of Michigan couldn't radiate more power."

EDWARD W. FISKE, education editor for the *New York Times*. 1992.

"The Harvard of the West."

HILLARY RODHAM CLINTON. U of M commencement speech. May 1, 1993.

Upper Peninsula

"Too far from civilization to ever amount to anything."

An unknown complainer expressing his unhappiness over Michigan getting the Upper Peninsula in exchange for giving up its claim to Toledo. 1830s.

"It's God's country all right. So few people live there that God alone looks after it."

A Michigan settler from the 1830s.

"(A) region of perpetual snows — the ultima Thule of our national domain in the North."

SHELDON McKNIGHT, editor, *Detroit Free Press*. 1836.

"A wild and comparative Scandinavian tract — 20,000 square miles of howling wilderness on the shores of Lake Superior."

Michigan Gazetteer. 1837.

"Andrew Jackson's left-handed gift to Lansing (in 1837) in return for surrendering Toledo to Ohio."

LOREN ESTLEMAN. *Downriver*. 1988.

"Siberia of Michigan.
Of this portion of Michigan, very little satisfactory information is to be had, and that which is known, is of a character devoid of much interest."

JOHN T. BLOIS. *Michigan Gazetteer*. 1838.

"Nature never contemplated such a union. ... a divorce from our unnatural partner is the only true mode of redressing the many evils to which we are subjected."

ABNER SHERMAN, in an essay calling for separate statehood for the U.P. 1858.

"North of the Straits is Hell."

A railroad supervisor's warning to an engineer charged with laying out a railroad route across the U.P. in the 1860s.

"The inhabitants of this region are in the position as the crew of a ship caught in the ice of the polar seas and forced to hibernate. Their winter is terrible."

COLONEL CAMILLE PISANI's observation while on a cruise of Lake Superior. 1861.

"Will someone inform the Gazette what earthly use the Lower Peninsula is to the Upper Peninsula, geographically or otherwise."

Portage Lake Mining Gazette. 1871.

"The country is fairly stewing in its own richness of resource."

WALTER NURSEY. *The City of Escanaba*. 1890.

"Italian skies and northern sunsets, rendered famous by the pens of poets and letters of traveled dilettantes, do not surpass, and I doubt if they could equal, the depth, beauty and purity of our Superior skies, while the intensity of our northern sunsets, as they illuminate the horizon with a crimson glory, are a fitting close to the days made perfect by an atmosphere purified by the mountains, by the vast unsalted seas, and by an almost unexplored wilderness of pine."

HEMPSTEAD WASHBURNE. 1890s.

"Michigan is two states. The Northern peninsula is cut off from the southern, physically, industrially, and in the history of settlement."

FREDERICK JACKSON TURNER. *The Frontier in American History.* 1920.

"It is one of the prettiest places in the world."

HENRY FORD. 1920s.

"Nowhere, probably, on the continent is fall foliage more beautiful in brilliancy or contrasting colors."

GEORGE SHIRAS. *National Geographic.* August 1921.

"Truly, it is a country of forlorn hopes, of ghost towns that never will come back but whose old residents, remembering the great days, cling to a hope; a country of railroads that never quite got built, or ore docks that burned and were not reconstructed, of veins of gold that petered out, of yawning holes in the ground into which men dumped millions before they would admit the ore just wasn't rich enough."

JOHN MARTIN. *Call it North Country.* 1944.

"Beyond the Straits of Mackinac lies a big, dark, lonely country few Americans can think of without emotion."

WALTER HAVINGHURST. *Land of Promise.* 1946.

"... Earth's most remote back 40."

JOHN GAGNON. *Detroit Free Press.* March 14, 1993. The reporter was recalling his childhood in the U.P. in the 1950s.

"The U.P. is a wild, harsh and broken land, rubbed and ground on the relentless hone of many past glaciers, the last one, in its slow convulsive retreat, leaving the country a jumble of swamps and hills and rocks and endless waterways."

JOHN VOELKER. *Anatomy of a Murder.* 1958

"Many modest cities have larger populations than the whole U.P., a forgotten region which was virtually ignored in the westward surge of population.

The simple truth is that the U.P. is one of the best hunting and fishing areas in the United States. It possesses three of nature's noblest creatures: the ruffed grouse, the white-tailed deer, and the brook trout."

JOHN VOELKER. *Trout Madness.* 1960.

"Up my way old township politicians never die; they merely look that way. Instead they become justices of the peace. It is a special Valhalla that townships reserve for their political cripples and has the following invariable rules of admission: The justice of the peace must be over seventy; he must be deaf; he must be entirely ignorant of any law but never admit it, and, during the course of each trial, he must chew — and violently expel the juice of at least one (1) full package of Peerless tobacco."

JOHN VOELKER. *Trout Madness.* 1960.

"... that land of wonderful wilderness."

EDWIN WAY TEALE. *Journey Into Summer.* 1960.

"... a step child of modern Michigan."

NEAL PEIRCE. *The Megastates of America.* 1972.

"Upper Michigan taught us many lessons in how to endure dashed hopes."

DAVID OLSON. *Life on the Upper Michigan Frontier.* 1974.

"Michigan's 'Dark Peninsula' had been dumped like a rich jewel between two of the Great Lakes. ..."

JOHN J. RIORDON. *Dark Peninsula.* 1976.

"If it weren't for U.P. winters, I would probably have never written a book."

JOHN VOELKER. *National Geographic.* June 1979. Under the pen name of Robert Travers, the former Michigan Supreme Court justice wrote numerous books, the most popular of which were *Anatomy of Murder* and *Trout Madness.*

"... it is an edgy place. I mean in the sense that it still hangs on out there like a rawhide flap of the old frontier, outposted from the swirl of mainstream America.

The U.P. is a hard place. A person has to want to hurt a lot to live there.

The U.P. is not the worst place in America to be a farmer nor is it the best. Some years, the growing season seems to be over the day after it begins."

JOHN G. MITCHELL. *Audubon Magazine.* November 1981.

"... a lot of young people have come to the U.P., moved by an honest appreciation of nature and the willingness to take any kind of job in order to be able to stay here."

JEFF GIBBS. *Mother Earth News.* January/February 1983.

"... perhaps the least-known land mass in the United States."

JIM HARRISON. *Sundog.* 1984.

"The story of how the Upper Peninsula finally became a part of Michigan must have made the angels weep. And doubtless also giggle."

JOHN VOELKER in the "Forward" to *They Left Their Mark* by John S. Burt. 1985.

"In the winter we shovel snow and in summer we swat mosquitoes. During the spring and fall we rest up for swatting and shoveling."

PETER OIKARINEN's reply to the often-asked question of Yoopers, "What do you people do up there?" 1987.

"What this glacially raked peninsula grows best is wood and rock."

TED BAYS. *A Most Superior Land: Life in the Upper Peninsula of Michigan.* 1987.

"The big thing I love about it is that the place is still so beautiful and empty of people that its scattered towns are little more than occasional scars and ax blazes between woods and endless waterways that run on and on for miles."

JOHN VOELKER. *Michigan Living.* April 1990.

"Now, me, personally, I like plaid because I am from the Upper Peninsula, where plaid is the official state color. However, when you mention plaid to women of non-Yooper descent, they often screw up their faces like they just smelled something bad."

ANDREW HELLER. *Flint Journal.* September 9, 1991.

"In many ways the Michigan Upper Peninsula ... is a world unto itself, like the Old World of the nineteenth century."

CLARENCE A. ANDREWS. *Michigan in Literature.* 1992.

"People in the U.P. really believe they have perfected life."

ROGER McCOY, Channel 50 (Detroit) newscaster, during a WJR (Detroit) radio "Focus" interview the week of January 1, 1993.

"The U.P. is small-town America, everywhere. It's the speed we move at — slow. It's circa 1950 up here. It's like you pass through an invisible barrier when you get over the bridge."

JIM DECAIRE, a resident of Ishpeming. *Detroit Free Press*. July 25, 1993.

"There's two things that keep people out of the U.P. The bugs in the summer, the snow in the winter. Otherwise, this would be worse than New York City."

FRED RYDHOLM, a long-time U.P. resident, teacher and author. *Detroit Free Press*. July 25, 1993.

Place Name Index

From the Pens of

The Author

Tom Powers, a lifelong Michiganian, has written three previous books, all descriptions and guides to Michigan's natural wonders and attractions. This book is a direct result of a Michigan history course he was required to attend as a fulltime student at Central Michigan University during the early 1960s. Powers had already developed a love of Michigan's great out-of-doors, but it wasn't until he took the mandatory class that he reluctantly realized his state's past was as interesting as its natural attractions. That forced introduction led to a passion for reading about Michigan's history and, later, mining marvelous quotes about the state.

When not reading, writing or traveling, Powers can be found at the Flint Public Library, where he is currently Supervisor of Services to Adults and Outreach. Powers hastens to point out that his 25-year career at the library deserves no special recognition but is instead a sterling example of one of the first laws of physics — a body at rest tends to stay at rest.

Tom and Barbara, his wife of nearly 30 years, have two children, three grandchildren, two dogs, a cat and a mortgage.